ALEPH-BET SOUP

Charles J. Thurston, MD

ILLUSTRATED BY ANDREW THURSTON

©March 19, 2000 & June 22, 2007 (Pocket Edition)

Library of Congress Catalogue # TX 7-559-773

D1545830

Printed by Southwest Radio Ministries, 2023

Table of Contents

Foreword

ALEPH-BET SOUP is a unique and exciting approach to the basic Hebrew and Greek biblical text. Dr. Thurston's easy-to-understand analysis brings to light a richly balanced King's Feast that beckons us to come and dine at the Master's table. In this book you will enjoy nibbling at the many examples of delicious revelations deciphered from the ancient texts, which you may have suspected were there, but that seemed to be tantalizingly just out of your reach.

As you read through these magnificent pages of deeply spiritual enlightenment, you will discover the awesome Word of God explained in a manner that is unequaled in the literary field of Bible codes. Dr. Thurston, utilizing his medical expertise and his unique and witty style of presentation, takes you step by step through his analysis of the Bible in such a delightful way that even a child could understand this subject matter.

You have heard the saying, *if you are sick or weak in body, eat a bowl of chicken soup,* but I say, if you are weak or sick in the spiritual realm, consume **ALEPH-BET SOUP** for a delight to your soul that will bring complete healing

to your inner man. Dr. Thurston's brilliantly composed book is a well-balanced meal of spiritual vitamins and minerals, bringing nourishment and new life to your thirsty and hungry soul. It was inspired by his deep love and holy respect for the Word of God. The mini lesson below should help you understand one of many reasons why Dr. Thurston has a passion for the Holy Scriptures.

The Hebrew Aleph-Bet comprises twenty-two letters. This equates to the astonishing fact that the human body also is designated with twenty-two amino acids, all of which are vital to a healthy and productive life on earth. The biblical Hebrew text, which uses those twenty-two letters, is precisely written with a uniquely interwoven mathematical system; yet it retains a poetical and musical sound as you listen to a fluent speaker of the language. Its message is consistent throughout, as it invites the reader to linger at the Master's buffet table of spiritual insights, eating and digesting soul-satisfying thoughts of eternal life.

Finally, I encourage you, dear reader, to consume this wonderful, spiritual food with an attitude of open-mindedness and a hungry, searching heart. So, let us sit down together at the Master's table, relax, and sip our Aleph-Bet Soup. It is for you, because it is just what the doctor ordered!

In Psalm 34:8, the Lord admonishes us to taste of Him. "*O taste and see that the Lord is good: blessed is the man that trusteth in him.*"

— Yacov Rambsel

Figure 1. Author & Yacov Rambsel

Prologue

Because my home had burned on February 7, the text of this book was finished at 8:00 PM, Sunday, March 19, 2000 AD in the basement of my parents' house. Only seven minutes later, at 8:07 PM that same Sunday evening, my mother, Erma Grace Thurston, went home to be with the Lord. She died following a long and heroic battle with a brain tumor. On the previous Tuesday she

Erma Grace (Jenkins) Thurston
1929-2000

had suddenly stopped eating and by the next day she could no longer even swallow water. Jesus said that he was the Bread of Life, and the Living Water. Just as God breathed the Breath of Life into Adam at the first so also did my mother's breath leave her at the very end. As all my sisters and my father stood around her deathbed and watched mom breathe her last I was suddenly aware of the curse of the Law and the penalty of sin portrayed in her frail body expiring before me. It was then that the Spirit of the Living God came into that room and made the dead text of this book alive. He showed me that without her spirit my mother's body had become a consonant, a clanging, empty bell that we would commit back to the elements of the earth. She was as absent from her body as the Holy Spirit is from the dead pages of any unread bound book. But she is now present with the Lord though absent from her body. I would like to dedicate this book to my mother, Erma Grace Thurston born to E. Ray and Myrtle Jenkins August 1, 1929.

The text of this book or any book is as dead as it can be unless it is read aloud and committed to the active memory banks of living people. The Hebrew Old Testament deadly curse of the Law was written only in consonants without the breath sounds of any vowels. The last word of that consonant-filled Testament is "curse" ם ר ח, CheReM. That is why the New Testament is written in Greek, a language with both consonants and living, breathing vowel sounds. The Old Testament contains the facts about what happened after the Fall of mankind and our penalty. The New Testament is about why we sin and how the payment of our legal debt was made in the death and resurrection of the Lord Jesus Christ. Mom and I will meet again not because we were religious, or because we read our Bibles but because we accepted into our dying bodies the gift of Eternal Life through Jesus Christ our Lord and became siblings with the first begotten from among the dead, *Jesus The Messiah*. I would invite you to join us at the end of time for a little get-together with our Creator, *Yeshua ha Mashiach,* ח י שׁ מ ה ע ו שׁ י . Jesus The Messiah.

This Prologue was originally written as the Epilogue in the first edition of this book because it illustrated the consummation of the spiritual vowels and the killing consonants. I have inserted it here at the beginning because it is also the heart of the matter and to show you what is in store ahead as you read. When you have finished this book, return to this page and revisit what you may have picked up along the way. The only two English letters with dots, "i & j", appear below. Salvation and eternal life are bound together in these two little letters. Why these two English letters are still dotted today originated in the Hebrew "jot" of Matthew 5:18. This is only one of the many mysteries we will solve as we look into the Hebrew letters.

After you have read the rest of this book, return to this Prologue to better appreciate the significance of these powerful dotted letters.

Aleph-Bet Soup

Introduction

Hebrew!? Oh No! Not Hebrew, Please!

Do not panic yet. Please remain calm! It is not necessary to become a Hebrew scholar to understand the Bible or this book. In fact, this book is mostly written in English, about English things by a Gentile. See! Right now you are reading that old familiar English your mother used to read to you when you were a child. The Hebrew writing at the top of this page is just the Hebrew *Aleph*-Bet. (Sounds nearly the same as the word *Alpha*-Bet, right?) It will not harm you in any way. These strange ancient symbols appear here and now in your life because there are some really neat insights into the Bible that become clear only in the word pictures of the Hebrew letters. These very English, very scientific and very inspiring insights found only in the pictures of the Hebrew letters may be easily appreciated without **any** further knowledge of the scary details concerning pronunciation, syntax, or any boring rules of grammar and the like. Rather than skipping over these foreign symbols as the lesser angels of our nature might encourage us to do, just think of the Hebrew squiggles as pictures and read the English words around them as captions and nobody will get hurt. Just step carefully over this next line of all the Hebrew letters and proceed into the timeless language of the Bible. They do not bite.

א ב ג ד ה ו ז ח ט י כ ל מ נ ס ע פ צ ק ר ש ת

What is So Special About Hebrew?

According to the great English Hebraisist and lexographer, Rev. John Parkhurst, in the introduction to his first Hebrew-English Lexicon of 1768, Hebrew was clearly the first language spoken on this earth between Adam and God, six thousand years ago[1]. Hebrew was the original language of the Word of God in the Old

Figure 2 Rev. John Parkhurst 1728-1797

Testament. It is still the only language to have survived from the ancient world without its own geographic country for the last two thousand years of the Jewish Diaspora. That great exile of the Jewish people is now coming to a close in our own time. Their everyday speech remains today as a plain and specific language composed of only about a hundred thousand ancient words. Compared with the nearly one million native, borrowed, and technical words that make up the massive and relatively promiscuous lexicon of the modern English language[2] the Hebrew language should be ten times simpler to learn than English.

Hebrew is an ancient Semitic (**Shem**-itic) language. Even if you do not buy Rev. Parkhurst's assertion that it dates back to the Garden of Eden, Hebrew clearly does date back to the Flood of Noah. It is a language inherited according to the Bible from a time at least as far back as **Shem**, Noah's eldest son. Following

---

1   Parkhurst, John Rev. 1728 (Julian Calendar)-1797 (Gregorian Calendar) A Hebrew-English Lexicon 1st Ed. 1762, 3rd Ed. 1823 William Baynes & Son Paternoster Row, London, England pp. viii Preface 3rd paragraph.

2   **The Story of English** PBS broadcast companion book **by Robert McCrum, William Cran, Robert MacNeil, Penguin Books 375 Hudson St. New York, N.Y. 10014 © 1986-1993 ISBN # 01401.5405 1**

the Great Flood of Noah about 2448 BC[3], Shem fathered the bloodline of all the Jewish and Arabic peoples. Shem was the eleventh generation from Adam in the genealogy of the fathers who were included in the ancestry of Jesus the Messiah. Shem's great grandson, Eber (Gen. 10:21), is called "Heber" in Luke's genealogy (Luke 3:35), and was likely the first He-brew[4]. Heber's great-great-great-great grandson was the most famous Hebrew ever, Abraham. He was famous for being willing to sacrifice his son, Isaac, and famous for Isaac's son, Jacob, also known as Israel. It was the twelve sons of Jacob who became the twelve tribes of Israel. Out of one of those tribes, Judah, came both Jesus the Messiah and the name of the Jewish people, the people of the Book.

Hebrew is the language of the people of The Book. It is as valuable for anyone to know how to read the street signs in the Holy Land as it is for any tourist or native  wandering through the Bible to be able to navigate its words and accounts in their original form and context. Each new insight that we may encounter in our tour of the Hebrew letters will make us all just that much more people of The Book as well.

---

3   Ussher, Bishop James, Bishop of Armagh, Ireland <u>Annals of the World</u> 1658 AD. Naïve? Maybe. Disproven? Not so far, and it's been nearly half a millennium.

4   No, "He-Brew" is not the national beer of Israel. It is interesting that a "beer" ר א ב is a well such as the well, Beer Sheba ע ב ש ר א ב , in Genesis 21:31 where Abraham and Abimelech swore an oath over a cold one.

Chapter 1
The Tower of Babel

א ב ג ד ה ו ז ח ט י כ ל מ נ ס ע פ צ ק ר שׁ תּ

This is a book written in English about the symbolism of the Hebrew letters in the Bible. That this encrypted symbolism exists at all is an example of a language barrier that has kept kindreds and nations, peoples and tongues divided on this planet for all of recorded history. In fact, the methods all people have used to record history have mostly been designed to conceal the less admirable parts of their own story. Secular anthropologists and biblical scholars alike all disagree about where a thing we call "civilization" began. Some say that civilization arose and moved out of Africa. Others contend for Europe or Asia. Each new study seems to reflect the ethnocentric prejudices of its author, but the preponderance of all the evidence encircles the Middle East as the cradle of civilization. The ultimate consensus points to the Middle East as the common source of civilization and recorded history. It is called the **MIDDLE** East simply because it is in the middle of everything on earth and is the centerpiece of history. We now know by satellite imagery and careful land surveys that the lands of the Bible are at the geographic center of the landmass of the earth. It seems most reasonable that God would start His Genesis Reproduction Project at the center of the landmass of the earth and expand it outward all over the earth. This is just as the science of anthropology has proven must have been the case.

In Genesis 11 the Bible records that mankind refused to spread out over the earth after the Great Flood of Noah. God came down and broke up that rebellion when He confounded the languages at the Tower of Babel. The language barrier that resulted at Babel has kept the rebellion of mankind against his Creator under control ever since. It marked the beginning of all the great migrations down from Mt. Ararat and out of the Middle East so well documented by nearly every anthropologist, archaeologist, and historian down through the ages. That dispersion unfortunately also marked the beginning of our fear of Hebrew and our estrangement from the original language of the Word of God[5]. We need to return to our linguistic roots in a unity with each other that is subject to the authority of God in order to truly see the biblical principles we are about to examine.

---

5   Isaac Mozeson in *THE WORD, The Dictionary that Reveals the Hebrew Sources of English* suggests that as many as 22,000 English words have Hebrew roots.

The True Origin of Languages

Before we dig any deeper into the roots of modern and ancient languages it is important to note that there is a fundamental difference between the evolutionary worldview and the biblical perspective of language. The secular skeptics, who view their evidence through the evolution-tinted glasses of the great rebellion of mankind, imagine the gradual development of language from primitive grunts up into our present-day worldwide literature and Internet speed-of-light-dot-com communications. They want to place the development of alphabets and phonics at the pinnacle of mankind's supposed evolutionary progress up out of grunts and cave pictographs[6].

---

6   Fred & Barney's artwork above is actually one of the oldest cave paintings in Lascaux France. On the next page note how this ancient painting depicts the stars of the Bible that would be present in the noontide darkness over Calvary at the Crucifixion. It clearly shows Sirius, Orion's belt, Taurus, & The Pleiades in iconographic precision.

The Sky of The Crucifixion
Stars Most Mentioned in the Bible

The biblical view, on the contrary, says in John 1:1, *"In the beginning was the word..."* It was the breath of God's word that spoke the worlds into being. Complex language came first not only as the horse pulling the little cart of civilization along but also as the director of the entire cosmos calling it into being.

Psalm 33

[6] *By the **word** of the LORD were the heavens made; and all the host of them by the **breath of his mouth**.*

Hebrews 1

[3] *Who being the brightness of his glory, and the express image of his person, and upholding all things by the **word of his power**, when he had by himself purged our sins, sat down on the right hand of the Majesty on high;*

Hebrews 11

[3] *Through faith we understand that the worlds were framed by the **word** of God, so that things which are seen were not made of things which do appear.*

The power of language, the precision of words, and the specifics of letters, alphabets, and numbers were given directly from our Creator, God, to Adam in the very beginning. Using these literary skills, Adam could name all of the animals. Could you name all the animals? How would anyone name all animals without writing the names[7] down? Despite the rather arrogant assumption of modern skeptics that all languages must have developed from simple into more complex forms way back in the hidden mists of so-called "prehistoric" time, we have no actual inscribed evidence that any major ancient language ever had those supposed early grunting, nouns-only, primitive developmental stages. All of the original languages, and all ancient writing sprang fully formed onto the scene no more than about five or six thousand years ago. Egyptian hieroglyphics were fully formed with complete parts of speech as far back as they can be traced. Sumerian pictographs and Cuneiform, Mayan glyphs (many still undecipherable) and even some modern railroad underpass graffiti[8], are recognizable as a complete set of complex phonetic symbols and the cuneiform writing of Assyrian and Babylonian cultures is found fully formed with a complex grammar and standard spelling conventions already embedded.

That there have been isolated enclaves of deteriorated and simplified language in so-called "primitive" societies throughout history and in the far reaches of the earth in no way proves that language or writing evolved from those remote degenerated cultures at all. It is rather what you might expect to have happen to a pristine original language in the hands of corrupt and sinful mankind. The fact that one culture copies from another does not contradict the fact of the dispersion at the Tower of Babel.

---

7   (I suspect that the names given to all the animals were composed by both Adam and his wife, Eve. At least it explains why half of the nouns in nearly every other language on the planet are masculine and the other half are feminine.)

8   My personal favorite graffiti reads, *"Hooked on phonics worked for me."* in silver spray paint on the Marietta Rd. Railroad Overpass near Chillicothe, Ohio.

According to the Genesis 10, often called the Table of Nations, seventy basic tongues were driven to the four winds over the surface of the earth away from that infamous Tower. The facts are really quite simple.

1.) No gradual evolutionary progression from simple to complex grammar, spelling, vocabulary, or letter-forms can be demonstrated for any written languages of the ancient world.

2.) Written or "Recorded history" goes back only about five or six thousand years to Bible times.

3.) The "Middle East" is still called the "middle" because it was the central location out of which all nations and kindreds and tongues emigrated to the ends of the earth.

4.) Mesopotamia[9] (as in "middle-potamia", or "between the rivers" in the Middle East) is called the cradle of civilization because that is where the dispersion of languages from the Tower of Babel originated.

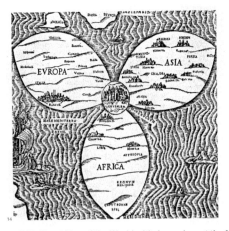

Figure 3 Medieval Map of the World with Jerusalem at the Middle

---

9   How do you fix a mess o' potamia and what do it taste like? Middle chicken?

Since the beginning of time Hebrew has been written in phonetic symbols just like all of the other languages on this planet. All languages came into sudden existence at the Tower of Babel. The forms of the phonetic symbols and letters have changed as much as we mortals have over the ages, but they have not improved any more than we as people or any other living things have. Although the basic phonetics have remained the same, even as we are still just as human today as Adam and Noah were, our written records and we are not as precise or as durable as the ancients were. When the original words were spoken in their pristine ancient form of the Hebrew language they were intended to be precise and truthful. This was necessary to record eyewitness[10] truth written in the Word of God from right to left over five thousand years ago. We have "developed" deteriorated forms of language such as slang, idioms, vulgarities, obscenities and profanities that confound and confuse the original meanings of words and phrases. Often these confusing idioms such as "Bad" for "Good" or "phat" for "thin and attractive" have been coined just to be "cool" or "hot" or just "cute". Modern slang and fashionable idioms have developed out of our inborn cultural dishonesty that tends to ratify rather than rectify our sinful nature.

Bob Dylan said it best, *"Well I don't know which one is worse, doin' your own thing or just being cool."*[11]

---

10 ת ו ל ד ו ת *Toledoth* is the Hebrew word translated *"These are the generations of . . ."* 11 times in the book of Genesis from which phrase it gets its English name. Each time it is followed by the name of the eyewitness who recorded what just preceded their signature: Jehovah in Gen. 2:4, Adam in Gen. 5:1, Noah in Gen. 6:9, Shem, Ham, Japheth in Gen. 10:1, Shem only in Gen. 11:10, Terah in Genesis 11:27, Ishmael Gen. 25:12, Isaac in Gen. 25:19, Esau in Gen. 36:9, and Jacob in Gen. 37:2. ת ו ל ד ו ת *Toledoth* is also the first word of the New Testament translated into Hebrew *"These are the **generations** of Jesus Christ"*.

11 1979 **Slow Train Comin'** Album *"Gonna Change My Way of Thinking"* [Author's note: Peace on Earth good will toward men was not a call to peace between "men of good will" or even between nations. It was rather a truce between an Earth in rebellion and the Kingdom of Heaven against which Earth still rebels. That Nativity cease-fire heralded by the angels culminated at Calvary in the terms of our unconditional surrender.

Since we are communicating about the Hebrew language in a deteriorated and contaminated (but of course, very cool) form of modern English it would be worthwhile to compare these two very different tongues.

English: The Tongue of the Great Rebellion

Our English language is a conglomeration of symbols from Hebrew and Greek alphabets, Latin and Teutonic grammars, romance words and phrases from Italian, French, and Spanish, and words and idioms taken from places like the Indus Valley to China and the South Pacific. The massive lexicon of the English language was gathered by; crusaders and monks, traders and brigands, sea captains and pirates over more than a thousand years. Modern English would be unintelligible to anyone from Britain only about eight hundred years ago. Remember the emotional trauma of reading **Beowulf** and **Chaucer** in school?

English is the modern *Lingua Franca* of international commerce, law, and transportation. It is the dominant language of diplomacy and the most likely foreign language to be found in other any other country. It is the language of Japanese air traffic controllers, of Italian harbor pilots, and of espionage in many non-English speaking police forces from Bombay to Timbuktu. It is also the language of world evangelization as well as the common denominator in United Nations talks. English is all of this and more because it is a relative newcomer on the world scene and it is the product of world exploration, evangelization, trade, and diplomacy from the great oceanic voyages of the Sixteenth Century explorers to the World Wars of this century. English has been freely assembled from the most popular languages on earth.

English has not been guarded from "contamination" as French, Italian, and Spanish have by the cultures and peoples that speak those Romance tongues. English is not as fastidious, nor as precise as Greek or Hebrew, but is more open to invasion, even "pollution", and compromise with all other tongues. It has become the most powerful force of world unification since the Greek language did the same for Alexander the Great and after him the Roman Legions in the ancient world.

I.N.R.I.

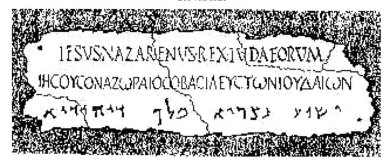

When Jesus was crucified, Pontius Pilate had ordered three signs to be placed over his cross; one in a form of Hebrew (Aramaic), one in Greek, and one in Latin. These signs were necessary to convey the accusation, *"This is **J**esus of **N**azareth, **K**ing of the **J**ews"* (Latin: **I.N.R.I.**)[12] to three different groups of people. That sign spoke to the local Jewish people in their native Aramaic, the Greek educated peoples who came out of the remnants of Alexander The Great's empire, and the official Roman garrison and legal system that would eventually make Latin the western world's tongue. These three languages have also dominated biblical thought throughout history. The Old Testament or Tanakh was written in the Hebrew of The Father God, the New Testament was written in the Greek of The Son's incarnation. St. Jerome's Latin Vulgate would be written in Latin, the dominant language of the Holy Spirit's future. That Latin Bible has been the dominant basis for most Bibles (including the King James Version) throughout Church history to the present.

---

12   Iesvs Nazarenvs Rex Iudaeorvm, John (19:19-20)

Those indictments over Calvary could also be classified into three representations of historical time; the first language, Old Testament Hebrew, from God the Father in what Hebrews 1:1 calls "*time PAST*"; Greek, the PRESENT cultural tongue of the Hellenized world in Jesus' day; and finally Latin, the language of "*these last days*" of the Holy Spirit in the FUTURE. The Roman Empire would eventually mingle its iron Latin grammar with the miry clay of ten other language toes in the feet of Daniel's prophetic image as history played itself out. Calvary marks the center of fulfillment of history now playing out before our eyes that had been foretold by prophets like Daniel half a millennium **B.C.**[13]

English: The Expected Feet of Clay in Daniel's Prophecy

Daniel the Prophet served in the Babylonian court of King Nebuchadnezzar during the seventy years of Israel's captivity from 586 BC to 516 BC. Daniel was able to reveal the lost dreams of King Nebuchadnezzar back to him along with their prophetic interpretations. In one dream, the king saw a great statue with a head of gold, arms and chest of silver, belly of brass and legs of iron standing on feet of clay mingled with iron.

---

13   We have chosen to rely on the historically time honored and very British sort of terminology of AD and BC rather than pander to the marketing interests of those who have only recently in the last century resorted to BCE and CE. We do not feel the need to *(subliminally)* emphasize the birth of Christ in the way that BCE and CE tend to do; Before or after the Common Era *(of that fellow, Jesus, we cannot mention)*. The year of our Lord Anno Domini and Before Christ seem so much simpler and more directly to the point. AD & BC also contain all of the first 4 letters of the Alphabet while BCE leaves out the **A**; which seems a bit unfair to the **A**. This is after all a book about all of the letters of the Alphabet, including the first letter.

Daniel 2

32 This image's head was of fine gold, his breast and his arms of silver, his belly and his thighs of brass,

33 His legs of iron, his feet part of iron and part of clay.

34 Thou sawest till that a stone was cut out without hands, which smote the image upon his feet that were of iron and clay, and brake them to pieces . . .

38[King Nebuchadnezzar of Babylon] *Thou art this head of gold.*

39 And after thee shall arise another kingdom inferior to thee, and another third kingdom of brass, which shall bear rule over all the earth.

40 And the fourth kingdom shall be strong as iron: forasmuch as iron breaketh in pieces and subdueth all things: and as iron that breaketh all these, shall it break in pieces and bruise.

41 And whereas thou sawest the feet and toes, part of potters' clay, and part of iron, the kingdom shall be divided; but there shall be in it of the strength of the iron, forasmuch as thou sawest the iron mixed with miry clay . . .

⁴³ And whereas thou sawest iron mixed with miry clay, they shall mingle themselves with the seed of men: but they shall not cleave one to another, even as iron is not mixed with clay.

⁴⁴ And in the days of these kings shall the God of heaven set up a kingdom, which shall never be destroyed: and the kingdom shall not be left to other people, but it shall break in pieces and consume all these kingdoms, and it shall stand forever.

The head of gold symbolized the Babylonian Empire set down in the Hebrew¹⁴ Scriptures by Daniel. The arms and chest of silver continued this empire statue with the divided arms of the Medes and the Persians until Alexander the Great's Greek language unified trunk and thighs of brass appeared in the middle of history reuniting the empire. The two legs of the iron Roman Empire depicted its eastern capitol at Constantinople and the western capitol at Rome. The iron legs stood on the mingled miry clay and iron feet of a divided Latin Holy Roman Empire. The feet and ten toes of mingled iron and miry clay represent our modern English world of international cosmopolitan travel and commerce. No wonder we have ten times the words of any other language; we are the ten toes. We are living in the last days of that prophetic image in the cosmopolitan feet of miry English clay. Bear in mind that these prophetic verses have been found intact in the Dead Sea Scrolls that clearly date from the First Century before Christ. Nebuchadnezzar's dream image was destroyed by a "stone cut out without hands" that many interpret as the re-gathered modern State of Israel cut out without force on May 14, 1948.

---

14   Yes, we know there is also some Chaldean and a heavenly bit on the wall about *MENE MENE TECKEL UFARSIN*. (**Thou art weighed in the balances & found wanting**) "**imminent doom or misfortune**" or "**the future is predetermined**".

The Great Battlefield of the English Bible

English is also the battleground in the translation of the Bible on a scale unparalleled in world history. There are more different English versions of the Bible (at least fifty) than any other translation in any other language. This variety has grown out of the numerous supernatural principalities and powers in high places engaged in their rebellion against our Creator. (We humans have helped too.) Satan and his minions have a greater vested interest in the English versions of Scripture than any other language in history if for no other reason than that more people are presently alive on this planet than have ever lived in all previous time. These spiritual enemies of the truth who have managed to warp and twist secular history into myth and legend have been especially frustrated since they have been effectively locked out of the original Hebrew and Greek texts by the extreme care with which Scripture has been handled by its Author and His "*holy men of old*" (all of whom were Jewish, by the way). The picayune precision and accuracy maintained by the Jewish scribes over the centuries is legendary. Not only has the Hebrew text of the Old Testament been hedged all around by the protective marginal notes in the Masoretic Text, it has an absolutely miraculous internal safeguard in the form of embedded codes of words, phrases, and numeric patterns like no other. There is no written record of any other people at any time in all history that even comes close to the embedded security and secret codes of Holy Scripture. The Bible codes and embedded numerical codes of the original tongues have not only served as a divine watermark authenticating the text but they have also prevented enemy tampering and falsification. No principality or any power on earth can disturb the sanctity and ancient integrity of the original Hebrew and Greek Scriptures because of the encrypted security codes found by the millions only in the Bible.

From time immemorial there have been brilliant men who have winnowed this pattern or gleaned that odd coincidence out of the arrangement of the words and letters on the pages of Scripture. The most famous attempts have been by the Jewish sages of the Middle Ages. The rabbinical sage, Rabbi Elijah Ben Solomon of Vilna (1729–1797), commonly known as the *Vilna Gaon* or the Genius of Vilna, found numerous **E**quidistant **L**etter **S**equences (**ELS**) that were buried within the surface text of the Hebrew Bible. Half a century ago Rabbi Michael Weissmandel of Prague assembled an immense collection of phenomenal "coincidental" embedded codes he found by hand in the Torah.

In 1976 Jerry Lucas and Del Washburn described a statistically significant mathematical pattern to the numerical value of words and phrases in the relatively loose Greek of the New Testament. They published their findings in a book titled <u>THEOMATICS</u>: *God's best kept secret revealed*. It was not widely understood because of its statistical basis.

More recently, since 1994 AD, hundreds of thousands of these embedded codes have come to light with the aid of high-speed computers.[15] We will look at some of these codes later once the basic letters of the Hebrew Aleph-Bet have become more familiar. For now, it is important to know that none of the embedded codes found in Scripture contradict the plain reading of the accounts, prophecies, promises, and commandments of the traditional surface text. Furthermore it remains impossible to predict the future with Bible codes, augury, astrology, or even authentic Messianic Bible prophecy. The future remains hidden from us until we get there, but the Bible contains in both the plain surface text and its numeric and equidistant letter sequence codes what we will encounter when

---

15   Doron Witztum, Eliyahu Rips, & Yoav Rosenberg of Hebrew University in Jerusalem published an article called *"Equidistant Letter Sequences in the Book of Genesis"* in the scholarly peer reviewed journal Statistical Science (vol. 9, no. 3) August 1994 pp. 429-483. More on this in Chapter 5, Reading Between the Lines.

we arrive at their future fulfillment. God will be there, waiting for us when we arrive in His future.

These embedded Equidistant Letter Sequence codes and numeric patterns present in the original language texts of Scripture were placed there in anticipation of the battle for the hearts and minds of our generation. We are on the front lines of an epic battle between our Creator and a creation in rebellion. The weapons have become much more potent in our own time with the explosion of instant knowledge and worldwide communications at the click of a mouse. The freedom of speech so treasured by the English both in Britain and its colonies in North America and Australia has permitted a very wide range of potential meanings of Scriptures not necessarily intended by The Author, as the Scriptures have been brought down to our modern lowest-English-common-denominator thinking. For it is not so much the original inspired Hebrew and Greek Scriptures that create divisive factions and such wide disagreements in theology. It is the inferior and imprecise nature of the English language spoken by sinful mankind uniting in rebellion today that engenders disagreement with Heaven. Our pluralistic modern society under the political correctness of cosmopolitan unity has permitted a much broader latitude of meaning not necessarily intended by the first Author of Scripture. It is this imprecision of English that compels our look back into the much more precise and narrow Hebrew words that served to keep the Bible mathematically perfect and the repository of untold secrets that only now are being revealed in these last days.

The Tongue of Shem in the Mouths of Ham and Japheth

Unlike English, Semitic languages read from right to left. Unlike the twenty-six letters of English or the twenty-four letters of the Greek Alpha-Bet, there are only twenty-two letters in the Hebrew Aleph-Bet. This should make it easier to learn, especially since these fewer letters are all consonants and they are all only upper-case letters. The vowels in modern Hebrew are supplied in the form of points or dots and lines that are salted around the consonant letters like seasoning as aids in their pronunciation. These modern vowel points appear in the following general fashion using X as a Hebrew Consonant:

a as in yacht, ה ת _ פ _ *Patah* X_ &	**e** as in stupefy ץ מ ק ף ט ה . *Hataf Qames* X
ץ מ ק . *Qames* X	**o** as in row, ם ל ו ה *Holem* X & iX
ee as in see, ק ר י ה . *Hireq* X & יX	**oo** as in zoo, ץ בוֹ ק . *Quibbus* X
ay as in hay, י ר צ .. *Tzere* X.. & יX..	& ק ר ו שׁ *Shureq* iX
eh as in bed, ל ו ג ס . *Segol* X	א ו שׁ The *Sheva* X☐

We will not worry much about Hebrew vowel pointings except to note that they exist in modern times as an aid to pronunciation. This table of vowel points may be found in Appendix VI in larger fonts. These vowel points were not present in the most ancient manuscripts such as the Dead Sea Scrolls and stone inscriptions. They were instituted as pronunciation aids after the temple service was cut off when Jerusalem was destroyed by Titus in August of AD 70 on the 9th of Av, the very day that Nebuchadnezzar destroyed the Ezra/Nehemiah-restored temple of Solomon over half a millennium earlier.

There are no lower case letters in Hebrew, but there are five final forms of the letters that appear differently if they are found at the end of a word. These letters served to separate words from each other in the original Hebrew text when there were no spaces between words. The following English sentence on the next page is written as if there were **FINAL** forms set in capital letters separating the words that run together like ancient Hebrew did.

thes**E**fina**L**form**S**ma**Y**hav**E**importan**T**m̈eaning**S**i**N** equidistan**T**lette**R**sequence**S**o**R**mathematica**L**patte rn**S**i**N**th**E**futur**E**

More plainly this would be written conventionally in modern form this way.

These final forms may have important meanings in equidistant letter sequences or mathematical patterns in the future.

Below is Psalm 19:1-2 with the final letter forms in larger **bold type and underlined**. In this example only Final Mem, **◌**, (versus regular **מ** form)[16] is present:

1.) ה ש מ י**ם** מ ספרים כ ב ו ד־אל

ו מ ע ש ה י ד י ו מ ג י ד ה ר ק י ע :

2.) י **ו ם** ל י **ו ם** י ב י ע א מ ר

ו ל י ל ה ל ל י ל ה י ח ו ה ־ד ע ת :

From Right to left above Psalm 19:1&2 read phonetically:

1.) Ha SHeMiY**M** MeSoFaRI**M** KeVOD-EL

(The heavens declare the glory of God)

VaMASeH YaDYaV MaGYD HaRaQYA

(The firmament sheweth forth His handiwork)

2) YO**M** L'YO**M** YaBYA OMeR

(Day unto day uttereth speech)

VaLYLaH LaLYLaH YaCHaVaH-DATH

(and night unto night sheweth knowledge.)

---

16   Final **Kaf ך** (vs. normal Kaf **כ**); Final **Mem ◌** (vs. normal Mem **מ**); Final **Nun ן** (vs. normal Nun **נ**); Final **Pe ף** (vs. normal Pe **פ**); Final **Tsadi ץ** (vs. normal Tsadi **צ**): Find the Mems **מ** above in the Hebrew Psalm that are not final. Hint: (they occur twice: **א מ ר ה ש מ י ם** &)

Please note that only five Hebrew letters have final forms that change their shape when they are found at the end of a word. These final forms only act from time to time as a hint to word breaks in the continuous lines of most ancient manuscripts. They exist for prophetic and symbolic purposes as well. For instance if you open up any Authorized King James English Bible at the back cover, from right to left, backwards, as if it were a Hebrew book you will find a remarkable fulfillment of a prophecy encoded in the architecture of the Hebrew letters. From Revelation, the last book of the New Testament, to the book of Romans you will count 22 epistles or letters to churches. The next book, Acts, is not a letter; nor are the four Gospels, John, Luke, Mark or Matthew. Of the 27 seven books of the Christian New Testament, 22 are letters, just like the 22 letters in the Hebrew Aleph-Bet, and five are histories found together as final forms if the New Testament is opened from the backside and read as if it were a Hebrew book.

The bottom line is that we do not have to worry about nearly as many rules or exceptions in Hebrew as we would in any other language. Ancient Biblical Hebrew has no vowels, no upper case letters, and there are only 22 consonant letters to learn. It is really not all that frightening. We will be comparing the twenty-two consonant letters of the Hebrew Aleph-bet with the other letters of more familiar modern symbols. We will find that most of the Hebrew letters are already well known to all English & Western readers in slightly different forms that we erroneously call the "Arabic Numerals"; but first, a "little Greek".

First A Little Greek

In order to ease the transition from our comfortable left-to-right familiarity with Western English into the right-to-left exotic language of the Middle East we might benefit from some examples of Hebrew letters in the more familiar left-to-right tradition of the Greek language first. Greek was one of the major contributors to English and, of course, served well as the language of the New Testament. The first two letters of the Greek Alpha-Bet are *Alpha* and *Beta* lending their names to make up the word *Alpha-Bet*, and gave rise to our English letters A and B. Similarly, the first two letters of the Hebrew Aleph-Bet are equivalent to our English letters A and B and have the vaguely familiar Greek sounding names of Aleph, א , and Bet, ב . The most ancient Phoenician form of the Hebrew letter Aleph actually looks like an upside-down English letter A. ⅄

The Bet, ב , looks very much like the number 2. It is shaped in the form of an enclosure that symbolizes the meaning of its name, "house", ב י ת ̤ Beit. The Moorish or Middle-eastern Sephardic pronunciation is '*Beit*' while the European Ashkenazi pronunciation is "*Beth*" as in "house of God" Bethel, א ל ̤ ‾ ̤ ‾ ב י ת , "house of bread" Bethlehem, ב י ת ̤ ל ̤ ח ̤ ם and "house of mercy" Bethesda. (Remember, Hebrew reads from right to left, so the Bet ב is on the right hand end of these words.)

Gematria γ = 3

The third letter of the Hebrew Aleph-bet is Gimel ג , and looks remarkably like our modern Arabic numeral **3**. It resembles the third letter of the Greek Alphabet, Gamma γ, and is the key to the etymological origin of the word "Gematria". Gematria is actually based on a Latin phrase, "*Gamma es trio*" or "*Gamma equals three*" and establishes a numerical value for every letter of the Alphabet in Greek. This number value also applies to Hebrew. In the ancient world before the invention of our familiar Arabic numerals; 1,2,3,4,5,6,7,8,9, and the zero, the ordinal position of a letter of the alphabet was written with a line over it to indicate that it stood for a number rather than a phonetic sound of a word. For instance in Hebrew, Aleph א stood for the number one, Bet ב stood for the number two, Gimel ג stood for the number three, etc. Therefore, every letter, word, phrase, sentence, or paragraph of any written language may also be assigned a number value based on the numeral assigned to each letter. The most familiar form of this number value assignment to letters is of course, Roman Numerals (where I=1, V=5, X=10, L=50, and C=100 D=500) [M was not used in the ancient Roman world. M is a modern contraction of two back-to-back C's that stood for 1000]. This principle of letters as numbers has been the basis for the art and science of gematria for thousands of years. The gematria of certain words and phrases bears a numeric symbolism that point to deeper spiritual, moral, prophetic or godly principles. Some of these are listed in Appendices I & II.

Fishers of Men
153 Fish & The Resurrection

After the resurrection, Jesus appeared to his disciples and many others on numerous occasions. The third such appearance of the risen Lord is recorded in the Gospel of John. Peter, James and John were fishermen who caught 153 fishes in their net in the days just after the resurrection of the Lord Jesus.

John 21

[10] *Jesus saith unto them, Bring of the fish which ye have now caught.*

[11] *Simon Peter went up, and drew the net to land full of great fishes, **an hundred and fifty and three**: and for all there were so many, yet was not the net broken.*

In the early, persecuted Church the symbol of a fish or the words "fish" in Greek ΙΧΘΥΣ or "fishes" ΙΧΘΥεΣ□ were used as secret codes that would identify the believers to one another. The fish sign also served to identify the church building, an example of which may still be found among the stone ruins of the 1st Century New Testament Church on Marble St. at Ephesus.

Each of the letters of the Greek word for fish, *I-Ch-Th-U-S*, IXΘΥΣ forms an acronym of the Trinity, XΘΥ, framed by the first letters of two different words for Savior, Iησουσ and Σατορ. These were all attributes claimed by the Lord Jesus Christ and are listed below.

Iησουσ, Iesous. Jesus means (Savior) from the Hebrew ‎שׁ ‎ו ‎שׁ ‎י , **Yeshua**.

Χριστοσ = Christos (Anointed, the Holy Spirit)

☐Θεοσ = Theos, God (Father)

Υιοσ = Huios (Son)

Σατορ (Savior)

Fish live in their water world just as we live our temporal lives on earth. A "fish out of water" was a sign of death and resurrection into the air out of the water for the earliest Christians. Jesus commissioned his disciples to be *"fishers of men"*. Peter, James, and John were fishermen who caught 153 fishes in their nets after the resurrection. This is a unique number with its own special personality. Although 153 is not a prime number as it is divisible by 3, it is still pretty special.

The pleural form of the "fishes" that the disciples were commissioned to catch inserts an Epsilon, ε, shown in lower case. The gematria of the Greek word *FISHeS*, (IXΘΥεΣ) (*Iota* I, *Chi* X, *Theta* Θ, *Upsilon* Y, *Epsilon* ε, *Sigma* Σ) is shown below.

(I)10 + (X)600 + (Θ)9 + (Y)400 + (ε)5 + (Σ)200 = 1224

An interesting "coincidence" is that 8 x 153 also equals 1224

The significance of this is that 8, the Dominical number often associated with the name of Jesus as shown below, multiplied times the number of fish in John 21:11 equals the gematrial number value for the pleural of the Greek word for fish as follows.

The name of Jesus in Greek is Ιησους (*Iota, Eta, Sigma, Omicron, Upsilon, Sigma*). The gematria of Ιησους is 888 and is calculated below.

I=10, η=8, σ=200, o=70, υ=400, ς=200.

10 + 8 + 200 + 70 + 400 + 200 = 888 or 111 x 8,

The Trinity (111) times the dominical number (8) is the numerical value of the name of Jesus. An eight laid on its side, as if dead, and raised up above the line as if resurrected is the symbol of infinity in mathematics. This symbol is taken from the Master Mathematician at His resurrection as the *First begotten from among the dead* and our promise of eternity.

It is certainly much more than chance that lead to a draught of exactly 153 fishes in the net. It is also beyond chance that the name of Jesus should have such a unique gematria that is associated with the "resurrection" of 153 fish, the number of dominion 8, the Trinity 111, and many other wonderful things some more of which are listed in Appendix II.

Although the gematria of the Greek word for "*fish*" and the symbolism of the number 153 have been common knowledge for centuries, the phenomenon of a pattern to these numbers in Scripture and prophecy was most thoroughly reported by James Harrison in his book **The Pattern and the Prophecy** [17] in 1996. It is the definitive work on the subject. An example of some of the more advanced and complex numeric symbols and divine watermarks of scripture may be found in **Appendix I**. *Number in Scripture.*

---

17   Harrison, J. **The Pattern And The Prophecy**, Fax (705) 741-1444
ISBN 0-9698512-0-0

The "*Stone cut out without hands*" of Nebuchadnezzar's dream in Daniel 2:34 may very well represent the sudden formation of the Nation of Israel by fiat of the United Nations on May 14, 1948. But there is another Rock that was not made with man's hands who resurrected from the dead and will return very soon to take possession of His Mountain Kingdom. It is that sacred Mountain Kingdom of Heaven that will topple the statue with feet of clay. In the next chapter we will get friendly with the letters of the language that will be spoken in that Mountain one day.

Chapter 2

Introduction to the Hebrew Letters

א ב ג ד ה ו ז ח ט י כ ל מ נ ס ע פ צ ק ר ש ת

Just as the Greek names for "Jesus", "fish" and "fishes" have numerical codes embedded within their spelling that link them together in resurrection and the trinity that establish their new Testament texts as the authentic Word of God, so also do the Hebrew words of the Old Testament have numeric place value and hidden codes sealing them. These buried codes are only now being fully resurrected in our time as yet another of the "many infallible proofs" that confirm the whole Bible as the very living Word of God. But to understand these proofs we must first get to know the characters of this ancient original text of the Hebrew Bible.

Tables listing the alphanumeric or gematrial number values of Hebrew and Greek follow. I have arranged these letters in three columns matching the Greek letters to their actual ancient numeric values with a similar system ***applied***[18] to the Hebrew letters. There are three columns; a column for ones, a column for tens, and a column for hundreds. Each column has nine rows. This arrangement of 27 letters is designed to help you see that the first nine letters of Hebrew א Aleph, 1, through ט Tet, 9, (and in the Greek chart A Alpha, 1, through Θ Theta, 9, etc. etc.) have numerical values in the Ones column: The next column is the Tens column, י Yod, 10, through צ Tsadi, 90: The last column is the Hundreds place value with the traditional values of ק Quof, 100, through ת Tav, 400. This arrangement of the Greek letters that permitted Greeks to count to 999, with each column holding a ones, tens, or hundreds place value may also be used to better remember the Hebrew letters.

Figure 5 Leonardo Fibonacci of Pisa

18   The five final forms ך Kaf, ם Mem, ן Nun, ף Pe, and ץ Tsadi, to the best of my knowledge **have never been assigned numerical values in the past**. They have been traditionally listed at the end of the Aleph-Bet however. I have assigned them the **potential** numerical values of 500, 600, 700, 800, and 900 in the pattern of the Greek alphabet to show that there is **potential** for counting to 999 with this system. I have no information that this was ever a convention in the past. I have include it here primarily as a memory aid for the Aleph-Bet. C. J. Thurston, M.D.

Gematria & The Hebrew Aleph-Bet		
ONE'S (1-9)	TEN'S (10-90)	HUNDRED'S (100-900)
(A/E) Aleph א = 1	(Y/i/j) Yod י = 10	(Q) Quof ק = 100
(B) Beth ב = 2	(K) Kaf* כ = 20	(R) Resh ר = 200
(G/C) Gimel ג = 3	(L) Lamed ל = 30	(S/Sh) Shin שׁ = 300
(D) Daleth ד = 4	(M) Mem* מ = 40	(T) Tav ת = 400
(H) He ה = 5	(N) Nun* נ = 50	*Final Kaf ך = 500
(f/V/O) Vav ו = 6	(S) Samech ס = 60	*Final Mem ם = 600
(Z) Zayin ז = 7	(A) Ayin ע = 70	*Final Nun ן = 700
(Ch) Cheth ח = 8	(P/F) Pe* פ = 80	*Final Pe ף = 800
(T) Teth ט = 9	(Tz) Tsadi* צ = 90	*Final Tsadi ץ = 900

Gematria & The Greek Alpha-Bet		
ONE'S (1-9)	TEN'S (10-90)	HUNDRED'S (100-900)
(A) Alpha A α = 1	(I) Iota I Ι = 10	(R) Rho P ρ = 100
(B) Beta B β = 2	(K) Kappa K κ = 20	(S) Sigma Σ σ ς = 200
(G) Gamma Γ γ = 3	(L) Lambda Λ λ = 30	(T) Tau T τ = 300
(D) Delta Δ δ = 4	(M) Mu M μ = 40	(Y) Upsilon Y υ = 400
(E) Epsilon E ε = 5	(N) Nu N ν = 50	(Ph/F) Phi Φ φ = 500
(none) Stigma ς = 6	(X/Z) Xi Ξ ξ = 60	(Ch) Chi X χ = 600
(Z) Zeta Z ζ = 7	(O) Omicron O o = 70	(Ps) Psi Ψ ψ = 700
(E/h) Eta H η = 8	(P) Pi Π π = 80	(O/W)Omega Ω ω = 800
(Th) Theta Θ θ = 9	(none) Koppa o = 90	(none) Sampsi ϡ = 900

More Familiar Than You Ever Imagined

As ancient and mysterious as these foreign alphabets of antiquity may at first appear, they gave rise to a major portion of our more familiar modern English. In fact, you probably already know nearly half of the Hebrew Aleph-Bet just from using the so-called "Arabic" Numerals 1, 2, 3, 4, 5, 6, 7, 8, 9, and the number 10 with its famous zero. The Eleventh and Twelfth Century European crusaders brought this clever decimal place-value method of counting-notation back from the Holy Land as they returned home from their ill-fated Y-1-K pilgrimages to reclaim Jerusalem in a foolish bid to contrive a sooner return[19] of the Lord. These

---

19 Bumper sticker for your car: "Prophecy Happens". It just does, otherwise it wouldn't be prophecy.

clever new numeric symbols adopted from the Holy Land had been preserved, by their Arabian and Jewish enemies. This was an improvement over Roman numerals and the traditional use of the letters of the Alphabet as number symbols that had previously been in use throughout the remnants of the old Roman Empire by the relatively crude Europeans. Popularized by Leonardo Fibonacci of Pisa, these Arabic and Hebrew (or more properly Semitic) symbols and the introduction of the Zero made modern calculations and mathematics possible. Without these important symbols your income tax would have to be written in Roman numerals today. NASA, the Atomic Energy Commission, and the Nuclear Regulatory Commission would have the very devil of a time without their decimal notation zeros and all. Note the similarity in the shapes of eight of the first ten Hebrew letters with their corresponding Arabic numerals. (The 5th & 8th letters are the only exceptions in print but have similarities in cursive script.) Associating the Hebrew letters with their Arabic Numerals will ease the tension of this encounter with a strange and ancient culture.

א ב ג ה ה ו ז ח ט י כ ל מ נ ס ע פ צ ק ר ש ת

1	2	3	4	5	6	7	8	9	10
א	ב	ג	ד	ה	ו	.	ח	ט	י
Aleph	Bet	Gimel	Dalet	He	Vav	Zayin	Chet	Tet	Yod
A	B	G/c	D	H(e)	V(f)	Z	Ch	T	Y(ij)

1. The long diagonal slant central to the Aleph, **א** , resembles the Numeral 1 as if it were slanted to the left surrounded by two **י** Yods, top and bottom.

2. Bet, **ב** , looks like a 2. It just does, and that's all there is *two* it.

3. Gimel, **ג** , has the same three left facing prongs that characterize a 3. The name Gimel comes directly into English as the word "camel", which gangly beast it somewhat resembles especially when any camel is attempting to kneel.

4. Dalet, **ד** , looks like an opened-topped numeral four. An ancient Phoenician Dalet from King Solomon's era looks like a Greek delta Δ or a closed-top four 4.

5. He, **ה** , only resembles a 5 in modern script form (sorry, this is one of the two exceptions).

6. Vav, **ו** , is an inverted 6. This has always been an important number-letter symbolizing mankind in general. Revelation 13:18 (666)

7. Zayin, **ז** , resembles a 7. It just does.

8. Chet, **ח**, (This is the only other exception.) Not only does it not exactly look like an Eight, worse yet, it closely resembles and is often confused with the other weird letter, He, **ה** . Except that a Chet (pronounced "ket") is closed at the upper left corner while the He **ה** (pronounced "Hay") has the left upper corner un-joined to the upright left leg. The rabbis say this space between the top of the vertical left leg and the horizontal cross bar **ה** is to let the air out when it is pronounced ("H-Hay"). This distinguishes He **ה** from the closed top of the hard **ח** Chet (pronounced "ket"). Chet is important as the first letter of the Hebrew word for lives, "Chaim" familiar to those who may have heard the common Jewish dinner toast "to life", "La Chaim" **ל ח־י ים** . It is also found commonly as a talisman in the form of a brass good-luck

fetish for sale to tourists in the Middle East and Chet, ח, is often confuse in shape with the Greek letter Pi, π. Chet, ח however, is not the symbol for the ratio of a circle's circumference to its diameter. (3.142859…etc.) Sorry again, but every letter cannot be a perfect match with every Arabic numeral.

No, wait! On second thought, *ch*ET without the *ch* does sound a bit like "eight" and it is interesting that both 5 and 8 are numbers associated with grace and the name of Jesus in Scripture and the numerical symbolism of resurrection. It is much like when the Israelites were commanded to walk seven times around Jericho on the Sabbath while they only had to walk around once each of the previous six days. This apparently violated the Sabbath doing more work on that victorious 7th day than in any one of the other six workdays. Even as Jesus was criticized about healing and doing his own work on the Sabbath so God had His chosen people do the same at Jericho; all recorded in a book named "Salvation of God" the book of Yehoshua ע שׁ ו ה י we call "Joshua" after a form of the name "Jesus"; The Ultimate Exception that proves the rule. Jesus came not to cancel the law but to fulfill it.

9. Tet, ט, has the appearance of a curled-up 9 resting on its back.

10. Yod, י , is a smaller version of the diagonal in the first letter, Aleph א , indicating that a repetition of the first nine numerals has begun again. It is the root of our lower case i with its little "dot" which became the decimal "point" itself in the metric system and scientific notation as in Pi, π, (3.142859…etc.) above. Yod is the "jot" of "jot & tittle" that shall not pass from the Torah until all things be fulfilled (Matt. 5:18). It is the first letter of "Jehovah", ה ו ה י , the incommunicable name of the Living God of Israel ordinarily spoken as "Adoni" meaning "Lord". Yod is also the smallest of the Hebrew characters and stands for the tenth and least of all the commandments, "Thou shalt not covet".

The Last Dozen Letters

The remaining twelve letters of the Aleph-Bet are; Caph כ , Lamed ל , Mem מ , Nun נ , Samech ס , Ayin ע , Pe פ, Tsadi צ , Quof ק, Resh ר , Shin שׁ , and Tav ת , (along with the five final forms of Caph ך , Mem ם, Nun ן, Pe ף, and Tsadi ץ, that are written differently when they appear at the end of a word). Sorry, but these letters have no numeral counterpart. 10 out of 22 ain't bad though, especially since we only needed nine of them. These last twelve letters demonstrate their own unique phonetic personalities in their forms.

Like Egyptian hieroglyphs where the animal glyph faced in the direction to be read, Caph כ mimics the open mouth facing left making its "K" sound from right to left in the direction Hebrew and all other Semitic tongues are read. The English hard "C" has done an "about face" into the direction of left-to-right western languages.

Lamed ל looks like a licking tongue.

Mem מ depicts the rounded pursed lips enunciating "M" sounds.

Nun נ is nudging the pallet with its tongue to make "N" sounds.

Samech ס looks like an "S" draped over a circle.

Ayin ע looks like the "sometimes Y" vowel it inspired and mimics.

Pe פ, like the others, faces left in the direction of its pursed-lip speech.

Tsadi צ resembles a cross between both its "T" and "Z" sounds.

Quof ק has the tail of the Q it inspired attached to a deeper throaty Caph כ behind it.

Resh ר is the angular thrust of the jaw making an "r" that

we now see reversed in English except on the store signs for "Toys "R" Us".

Shin שׁ has much more about its character that we will see in the last chapter to make up for its lack of familiar western attributes.

Tav ת has a foot stuck out taping out "T" sounds from right to left. It is one of the three cross-shaped or "T" sounding letters in Hebrew: Vav, ו, the shepherd's crook that inspired our F, Tet, ט, the curled up 9 of judgment, and Tav, ת ; one for each of the 3 crosses at the Crucifixion.

The Letter of the Law & The Spirit Wind

There are no official vowels in the Hebrew Aleph-Bet even though four of the letters, Aleph א , Vav ו , Ayin ע , and Yod י , are sometimes supposed to be pronounced as vowels, the formal expiratory sounds, tones, or carrier vowel sounds have to be added to the consonants as Hebrew points today. The absence of vowels in English would cause this sentence to read more like this: "**th bsnc f vwls n nglsh wld cs ths sntnc t rd mr lk ths.**" This resembles teletype weather bulletins that abbreviated "thunderstorms" as "thndrstrms" with little or no confusion for those who were used to reading them but rendered an ordinary weather report unintelligible to the uninitiated reader. But man cannot speak by consonants alone.

The act of speaking or singing requires a carrier tone in the form of vowels such as A, E, I, O, U, and sometimes Y, which may be uttered at various **frequencies**, **wavelengths** and **amplitudes** (or loudness). These three qualities form a trinity governing the sound that persons make. Per-son is a combination of a prefix, Per-, that means "through which a thing passes" and the root "-son" which means "sound". We are living persons through whom the sound of the Spirit passes. This pneumatic, spiritual, breathing-hum is modulated by the clicking, guttural, tonguing effects of the consonants. "*Con*-SONANT" literally is Latin for "*with*-SOUNDS". None of the dead consonants of any language, including Hebrew, make any sound. They only interrupt, break, or divide and modulate the spiritual flow of existing vowel sounds. It is the consonants that assign the detailed meanings and specific abstract definitions that form words and language . . . and it is these dead consonants that compose the letter of the Law and give understanding to raw vowel emotion; For Hebrew, the factual language of the Torah or the Law, has no vowels.

Words, details, and legalities, are required because of the curse of the Law, and because we cannot live by bread alone in a world where even that bread comes at the expense of the sweat of our dying brow. It is the curse of death that is the power of the Law. That deadly threat of the Law is our schoolmaster until we depart this mortal coil. We praise God in hymns and songs and music with harmonies and emotion. The consonants cut into and cut off the flow of the spiritual vowel sounds to impart meaning and the specific points of the law "*. . . for the letter killeth, but the spirit maketh alive.*" (2 Corinthians 3:6) The Hebrew Torah is written in killing letters . . . all consonants, no written vowels. The Book of the Law was composed of killing consonants, stored in a coffin called the Ark of the Covenant. In that Ark were other mementos of death; objects such as Aaron's dead rod that budded and the pot of manna that is mentioned by the Lord Jesus in John 6:49, "*Your fathers did eat manna in the wilderness, and are **dead**.*"

Until the Temple at Jerusalem was destroyed in 70 AD by the Roman General, Titus, the spoken and chanted Word of God as recorded in the Hebrew Scriptures was commonly composed of unwritten but understood vowel sounds modulated by the written consonants. When the Temple form of worship was destroyed and its unwritten traditions, forms, and pronunciations of the vowel sounds were no longer passed on aurally from generation to generation, the vowel points came into being as vowel sound pronunciation aids. Although it could have been in use by the time the Lord Jesus noted the importance of the "Tittle", this vowel pointing was not firmly established until around 800 AD by the Masoretes. It may be seen today in the traditional manuscripts on which all of our modern Bibles are based. The much older Dead Sea Scrolls that were discovered in 1947 had no vowel pointing. The Dead Sea Scrolls were not vowel pointed because they were written while the oral-aural vowel-sound tradition could still be passed on from one generation to the next by living, breathing, and practicing Priests and Levites in daily Temple service. Living vowel pointing did not enter the written Hebrew language until after Calvary: Calvary, when the human race was saved from the very last word of the Old Testament, ם ר ח, CheReM, that means "a curse".

THE BIG PRINT FOREST

The Letters as Leaves Blowin' in The Wind

The Bible claims to be the very living Word of God and describes the nature of God in Trinitarian terms of The Father, The Son, and The Holy Spirit. "*And God said. . .*" or "*By the breath of His mouth . . .*" and many other phrases that pepper the text of the Bible indicate that God seems to have preferred the spoken word as His method of creating, sustaining, and intervening in His physical creation. The individual Hebrew letter symbols are like the little leaves of trees whose larger forest undulates in graceful waves moved by the harmonic wind of the Spirit of God. For God is Spirit and we worship Him in spirit and in truth. (John 4:23 & 24)

The musical, spiritual-sound-waves of any language, including Hebrew, have three properties that define them; their pitch or **frequency**, then the **amplitude** or intensity of that pitch or intonation with its associated unique **wave-lengths**. This Trinitarian set of vowel traits is then modulated by the twenty-two consonants that generally appear in sets of three letters of each Hebrew root word. The vast majority of Hebrew roots are composed of just three letters. There are a few roots with two letters and a few composed of four, five or six letters, but most are of exactly three letters that modify the three parameters of the vowel carrier waves. This Trinity is unique to Semitic languages that descended from Noah's oldest son Shem, "The Name". This is one set of examples of hundreds of trinities found in nature reflecting the Trinitarian character of our Creator-God. Here are a few three-letter Hebrew roots illustrating this three-ness in the Word of God.

א ב ד **ABaD**, work, broken, destroyed, etc; א ד ב **ADaB**, grieve; א ד ם **ADaM**, man, red, ruddy, low; א ל ה **ALaH**, curse, swear, execration, oath, lament; א מ ן **AMeN**, truth, amen, so be it, (I believe it); ב ר ח **BaRaCh**, flee, fly or shoot through: מ ל ך **MeLeK**, king, royal. י _ ד ע **YaDA**, to know as in intimate sexual knowledge as in *yada, yada, yada*[20].

So far we have learned that Hebrew has common properties with every other language on the planet. These include pictorial symbols called letters that stand for about twenty-two phonetic sounds. These abrupt **tongue, lip,** and **throat** stops are inserted into the musical spiritual flow of sound to give meaning to the music. The music is a trinity of **frequency, amplitude,** and **wave-length**

---

20   Jerry Seinfeld "knew" this intimate sexual characteristic when he popularized "yada, yada, yada" on TV.

that carries the sound of the words. Each phonetic letter in Hebrew is one of **three leaves** on a word twig of a phrase branch in the tree of sentences that is the forest of literature. These sentences are composed of a trinity of parts of speech; **nouns**, **verbs,** and **helpers**. Nouns are found in threes as physical **persons**, **places**, or **things** just as Jesus the Son of God came in physical flesh (a thing). Verbs power the sentence in three forms; **active**, **passive**, and **transitive** much like the power of the Father-God. Helper words like **adverbs-adjectives**, **prepositions**, and **conjunctions**[21] help to modify and clarify the other words like the Holy Spirit helps us in our daily lives. These trinities of trinities of trinities found naturally in the pattern of all language did not arise out of grunts and primitive moaning. These patterns of the Holy Trinity are commonly found in all language as a remnant of the unifying Hebrew of the world before the dispersion at the Tower of Babel. Today Hebrew seems strange and exotic to western eyes and ears but really has much in common with the relatively huge lexicon of the English language. You already know the first ten letters of Hebrew if you can count to ten. The other twelve look like the sounds they make. Since there are no vowels, no capitals, and only twenty-two letters in the Hebrew Aleph-bet, it is really much simpler to learn than any western Alphabet once the symbolism of the strange squiggles is understood.

In the next chapter we will discover that the first ten Hebrew letters you already knew from counting to ten on your ten digits all your life have a relationship to the Ten Commandments. We will also demonstrate an absolutely amazing correspondence between the first ten elements of the Periodic Table of the Elements and the symbolism of the first ten letters in Hebrew.

---

21   I know we promised not to delve into the rules of grammar etc. Terribly sorry to have resorted to parts of speech here. It will not happen again.

Chapter 3

The Ten Commandments

א ב ג ד ה ו ז ח ט י כ ל מ נ ס ע פ צ ק ר ש ת

Figure 6 U.S. Supreme Court Door Panel

The Hebrew word ל א , *EL*, means "power" as in "Almighty" and is synonymous with "God" as in the words *El Shaddai,* י ד שׁ ל א , or *Elohim,* ם י ה ל א , etc.. The "*E*" of *El* in these powerful words for God is transliterated into English from an Aleph, א , that is technically silent in Hebrew. But Aleph, א , may be thought of as implying nearly any vowel sound, A, E, I, O, & U, and sometimes Y, depending on the pointing or traditional pronunciation. Aleph is most often transliterated as an "*A*" or an "*E*" and rarely as an "*O*". Aleph was the first letter and came out of the mouth of God in His breath that created all things. Aleph is as inaudible as God is invisible; but if pronounced, א has the spirit-wind breath character of the vowels. All created physical things began at the imperceptible spiritual level and proceeded into existence as the hard consonants of what we call physical "reality".

The next letter of *"EL"* is Lamed, ל . It is a tongue-shaped pictograph of this lingual consonant's pronunciation.

In the poetry embroidered by God in His weaving of the Hebrew tongue, the reverse of א ל , EL, "Almighty absolute power", is ל א , LO, meaning "not", "none", "absolute absence" or "void". The message is clear. It is all, א ל (EL), or nothing, ל א (LO). Perhaps both the English words "All" and "No" came out of the EL and LO of Hebrew. The absence of God is the absolute definition of nothing and the beginning of anything and everything is always God. With this new understanding of the profound importance of these two simple letters their power may now be seen in the ל א "Not" or **"No"** or "Thou Shalt Not" shown in eight of the of the Ten Commandments listed in the columns on the next page, below.

The Ten Commandments (Exodus 20)

	א ל
I. No other Gods before Me	א ח ר י ם ע ל ⁻פ נ י י ה י ה ⁻ ל ך א ל ה י ם
II. No graven images	א ל ת ע ש ה ⁻ ל ך פ ס ל
	א ל
III. No Names taken in vain	א ל ה י ך ל ש ו א כ י ל א ת ש א א ת ⁻ ש ם⁻ י ה ו ה
IV. Remember the Sabbath to keep it holy	⁻ י ו ם ה ש ב ת ל ק ד ש ו ז כ ו ר א ת
V. Honor thy father & mother	⁻ א ב י ך ו א ת ⁻ א מ ך כ ב ד א ת
VI. No murder	ל א ת ר צ ח: ס
VII. No adultery	ל א ת נ א ף: ס
VIII. No stealing	ל א ת ג נ ב: ס
IX. No false witness	ב ר ע ך ע ד ש ק ר: ס ל א ⁻ ת ע נ ה
X. No coveting	ל א ת ח מ ד

What Part of

Do You Not Understand?

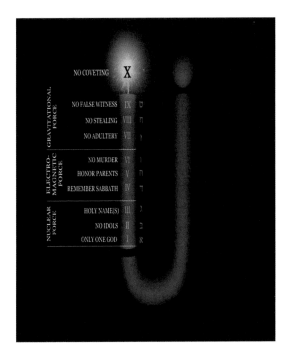

The Decalogue From Right to Left and Bottom to Top

Only ten of the 643 Levitical laws and regulations found in the Five Books of Moses ever really made the big time. Most of the educated human race has at least heard of the Ten Commandments. They are widely acknowledged as the bedrock of all Judeo-Christian morals, Greco-Roman laws and thereby the basis of every western constitution whether European, Russian, British, or Colonial. The Decalogue is the basis of all laws and of course the American legal system. No empire, or major civilization has ever dared to contradict the Decalogue and survive.

In recent years the legal insanity of some of the United States District Courts and the stupidity of the Alabama Supreme Court in removing Chief Justice Roy Moore over issues that focus on the Ten Commandments has placed the Decalogue in the headlines. Christians and Jews alike are passionate about the sanctity of the Ten Commandments, but very few of these fervent people can recite the Decalogue from memory. Nobody can keep them. It is time to take a different look at these important commandments so that more people may be able not only to know what they are so passionate about but also that they may be able to keep these commandments. In order to get a better look at these important instructions it might be interesting to inspect them from below like an automobile up on the lift. We will learn them from the least to the greatest from the bottom to the top.

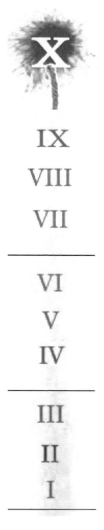

But many that are first shall be last; **and the last shall be first***.*

Matthew 19:30

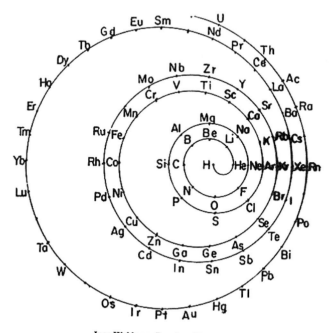

Ingo Waldemar Dagobert Hackh, 1914

Picture the Ten Commandments as a stick of dynamite standing upright on its base. Imagine the Tenth Commandment sticking out of the top as a fuse that can light off ever more explosive forces as the stick explodes from the least to the most offensive violations of the 9th through the 1st Commandments. The explosive forces of the Decalogue may be divided into weak gravitational or personal forces, stronger electrostatic or social forces and powerful nuclear or Divine forces.

This correspondence between natural and Torah law is more than just a handy literary device for comparison. There is an amazing correspondence between the Decalogue and that Periodic Table of the Elements that you may remember gracing the front wall of your high school chemistry classroom. The written Decalogue in the Word of God matches the first ten elements in the periodic table of the Works of God in nature. As we examine each Commandment we will also demonstrate its connection with the orderly structure of nature by noting its chemical element. The details of the specific parables of the elements and their relationship to the Decalogue and biblical number codes are all listed in **Appendix IV**.

PERIODIC TABLE OF THE ELEMENTS

The 10th Commandment

Element #10 [Ne] Neon, a Noble Gas (Appendix IV)

Symbolized by the least of the Hebrew letters ׳, Yod or Jot equivalent to English letters Y, ij and the "dot" (jot = dot) or period "."

X. *Thou **shalt not** covet . . .*

ד מ ח ת א <u>ל</u>

The least commandment was listed last in the Decalogue. Even though the least of the Ten, it remains unto this day as the short fuse that can light off the rest of the whole sinful stick of dynamite. It is retained even in our English letters by the little dot over both the i and the j and is masked by pride when we make our first-person personal pronoun a capital I instead of a lower case i. Coveting is a sin against no one else but the individual who is tormented by unfulfilled desires. Coveting is a personal sin that affects only the frustrated sinner, but is the motive that leads to the violation of all the rest of the Decalogue. That is why Jesus said in Matthew 19:19 to the rich young ruler who already retained many coveted possessions that he should sell all that he had obtained through covetousness and give it to the poor. Jesus was challenging the rich man's false claim that he had kept all of the commandments. James, the Lord's brother, wrote that he who has violated even the least of the commandments has violated them all (James 2:18). Yod ׳ is the little fuse that lights off the rest of the Romans-1-candle of sin.

The 9th Commandment

Element #9 [F] Fluorine, a Corrosive Salt (Appendix IV)

Symbolized by the Hebrew letter ט, Tet, equivalent to the cross-shaped English letter T.

IX. *Thou shalt not bear false witness against thy neighbor.*

ס : ר ק ד ש ד ע ך ע ר ב ה נ ע ת ־ א ל

Bearing false witness against a neighbor to their greatest harm occurs in a court of law at the seat of judgment. Nine is the number of judgment in Scripture. This is theft of reputation, a sin against another person not just oneself. Its Hebrew letter is retained in English by the cross-shape of the letter T, where the Lord Jesus bore our judgment for us.

Breaking this commandment steals a person's reputation. This is a devastating loss to the victim and of no personal value to the thief. Violation of the Ninth Commandment crosses the threshold from personal covetous sin into pointless violations against others as a form of malice.

The 8th Commandment

Element #8 [O] Oxygen, dOminion Breath of Life (Appendix IV)

Symbolized by the Hebrew letter ח, Chet, equivalent to an English "Ch".

VIII. *Thou shalt not steal.*

ס : ב _ נ ג ת א ל

Stealing the property of others usurps their dominion over their material worldly goods. Eight is the Dominical number, the number of the Lord who was raised from the dead on the Eighth Day. The Gematria of Ιησους, Jesus is 888. (10+8+200+70+400+200 = 888). The horizontal Eight ∞ is the symbol for infinity and 8 is the number of new beginnings in Scripture. ח Chet is the first letter of ChaIM, ם י י·ח _ , "Lives" (masculine pleural=All Lives).

Transgression of this commandment is theft of another person's dominion over their goods, and therefore involves the threat of theft for the rest of society making it not only a sin against one other person but against many others.

The 7th Commandment

Element #7 [N] Nitrogen, Protein Synthesis (Appendix IV & V)

Symbolized by the Hebrew letter ז , Zayin, equivalent to an English Z.

VII. *Thou **shalt not** commit adultery.*

ל <u>א ת נ א ף</u>: ס

Stealing another's spouse violates the sanctity of marriage and warps the rearing of the next generation of children. Giving birth, generating new lives, and gestation are accomplished in exact multiples of weeks (7 days) for all species that multiply by sexual reproduction. Bringing another nephesh ש פ נ or life into the world parallels the life giving work of the Holy Spirit. Seven is the number of spiritual perfection in the Bible.

This is a sin against not only others but more than one generation and at least two families. It has even more social impact than the other thefts of reputation and material goods already mentioned.

The 6th Commandment

Element #6 [C] Carbon Based Life Forms (Appendix IV)

Symbolized by the Hebrew letter ו , Vav, equivalent to English V, f, or O.

VI. *Thou shalt not kill.*

ל א ת ר צ ח: ס

Murder takes the life of another man. Six is the number of man; made on the Sixth day; who's hours of the day on this Earth are divided into four watches (the number of the Earth and its 4 corners, N.S.E.W.) of six hours each; we live three score (60) and ten years; Jesus the Messiah was crucified on a cross shaped like an ancient Phoenician form of the letter Vav ו according to "tradition" on Good Friday[22], the Sixth day of the week. "F" of Failure, is still the sixth letter in English and has negative symbolism even in school grading to this day in our culture. The sixth cardinal alphanumeric symbol in Greek is the specially inserted serpentine letter Stigma ς, and is preserved in its negative meaning in the stigmata of Christ or anything stigmatizing. The true sixth ordinal letter in Greek is Zeta, ζ also not unlike the shape of a coiled serpent, as the one Moses raised up in the wilderness (John 3:14). The Sixth commandment forbids the sin of murder against not only the victim but against permanently interrupting the flow of life down through the generations of everyone cut off in the future. Those that would have been fathered by the murder victim are also the victims of the killer. His offspring may have

---

22   Wednesday, April 5, 30 AD, 14th Nissan 3792 Crucified & died at 3:00pm "Betwixt the evenings" PM noon & Sunset 6:00 PM, Exodus 12:6. In the grave 3 days & nights like Jonah. Evening/Morning Thursday April 6, Friday April 7, Saturday April 8. Raised Hell Saturday night (Early Sunday April 9 Gentile). Sorry, there is no such thing as "Good Friday"

numbered even in the millions and his murder sealed the fate of every cut-off-generation that failed to be born when the murderer interrupted God's flow of the river of lives through the generations out over the surface the Earth.

Murder is a sin against the victim; a sin against the present generation who cowers in fear from the horror of it; a sin against the previous generations who bore the victim in vain; and a sin against the succeeding generations that will never be. This interruption of the flow of life makes murder also a sin against the future, as well as the past.

The 5th Commandment

Element #5 [B] Boron, a Gracious Flux or Neutral Soap (*20 Mule Team Borax* Appendix IV)

Symbolized by the Hebrew letter ה , He equivalent to an English letter H.

V. *Honor thy father and thy mother.*

ך מ א ־ ת א ו ד י ך ־ ב א ־ ת א ד ב כ

Honoring father and mother brings long days of life in the land granted by God. Five is the number of grace in Scripture. Charis, η Χαρις, Greek for the grace or the gift, has a Gematria that is a multiple of five (8+600+1+100+10+6 = 725) or (52 x 29) God's grace is shed from the heavens, Ha Shamyim, ם י מ ש ־ ה , who's

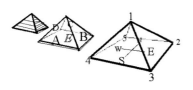

Gematria (40+10+40+300+5= 395) also is a multiple of five. The most gracious government we will ever encounter on the four corners of this Earth from anyone

is generally from our parents. God's gracious government is shed on our occupation of this Earth Ha'Eretz, ‏הָ ־ אֶ רֶ ץ‏ , the Gematria of which (90+200+1+5=296 or 4 x 2 x 37) is a multiple of four (and also eight, like Chet, ‏ח‏). Feel free to check these numeric values against the charts in Chapter Two.

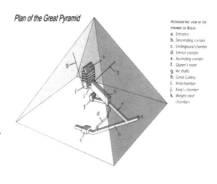

Plan of the Great Pyramid

AXONOMETRIC VIEW OF THE
PYRAMID OF KHUFU
a. Entrance
b. Descending corridor
c. Underground chamber
d. Service corridor
e. Ascending corridor
f. Queen's room
g. Air shafts
h. Great Gallery
i. Antechamber
j. King's chamber
k. Weight relief chambers

The Great Pyramid of Cheops on the Giza Plateau is defined by five points: the apex in the heavens shining its grace down over the four corners of its base on the Earth. It is a model of the northern hemisphere of the globe. It has five surfaces and most of its dimensions are multiples of five. The Cross of Calvary has five points, each tip and the intersection of both beams. It carried the body of the Lord Jesus with five piercing wounds; both hands and both feet as well as the spear wound in his side. The dimensions of Noah's Ark and the aspects of the Tabernacle of Moses are also in multiples of five. The Great Pyramid, The Ark of Noah, The Ark of the Covenant, The Wilderness Tabernacle and Calvary all represent God's grace shed from Heaven on the Earth to save us.

Failure to care for our grandparents will train our children not to care for us, as parents, and no one will be left to care for the elderly. This is an affront to our ultimate Father, God, with social ramifications now best illustrated in any nursing-home-warehouse where old, senile, and crippled parents are deposited by neglectful children to drain the coffers of society at a huge cost in money and an incalculable cost in suffering and neglect. If your parents are in a nursing home go visit them every day and take your kids along.

The 4th Commandment

Element #4 [Be] Beryllium, a rare earth element (Appendix IV)

Symbolized by the Hebrew letter ד , Dalet equivalent to an English D or Greek Delta Δ.

IV. *Remember the Sabbath day to keep it holy.*

ז כ ו ר א ת ־ י ו ם ה ש ב ת ל ק ד ש ו

Keeping the Sabbath is for man's rest and mankind's good as he keeps the earth. It applies only here on earth, where the other six days must be spent in toil. Four is the number of the earth with its four winds, four seasons, four compass points and four

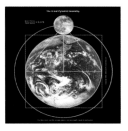

corners. The simplest three-dimensional figure, the tetrahedron, requires four points in space to define it. Labor on the Sabbath by one person demands labor by those who may have to tend his

work including; waiters, clerks to supply his food and supplies, surgeons and firemen to rescue him when he gets injured etc. It is not a sin against any one human being but against everybody else and God Himself.

The 3rd Commandment

Element #3 [Li] Lithium, The Rock (Appendix IV)

Symbolized by the Hebrew letter ג , Gimel equivalent to an English G or C.

III. *Thou **shalt not** take the name of the Lord thy God in vain.*

ש מ ־ י ה ו ה א ל ה י ך ל ש ו א כ י ל א
ל א ת ש א א ת

There are three names that we take in vain; Father, Son, and Holy Spirit. Three is the number of completeness as when a third side completes a plane geometric figure such as a triangle. While annoying and offensive to various other people among the pious and religious, it is really a sin against the three persons of the Godhead alone.

The 2nd Commandment

[He] Helium, The Sun's Noble Gas (Appendix IV)

Symbolized by the Hebrew letter ב , Bet equivalent to an English letter B.

II. *Thou **shalt not** make unto thee any graven image . . .*

ל ס פ ד ל ־ ה ש ע ת א ל

Any graven image is a second copy of the original. There are to be no copies of the Living God. Two is the number of division and difference in Scripture; Man & Woman, Cain & Abel, Jacob & Esau, Living & Dead, Sheep & Goats etc. In geometry two points define a straight line. _____ The ends of this line are said to be opposites. The line joins or marries these opposites. The points at opposite ends of this marriage line remain in opposition. One of the opposite ends of this line was the original point from which the line was drawn. But once drawn in space the opposite end point of that line, the copy of the original point, cannot be discerned from its original. Idolatry confuses the copy with the original Living God. This division and dilution of God as a graven finite image is a sin against God alone.

The 1st Commandment

Element #1 [H] Hydrogen, Deuterium, Tritium (Appendix IV)

Symbolized by the Hebrew letter א , Aleph equivalent to English letters A/E/O.

I *Thou shalt have __no__ other gods before Me.*

י ה י ה ־ ל ד א ל ה י ם א ח ר י ם ע ל ־פ נ י
ל א

One God excludes any other counterfeit "gods". One is the number of unity. In geometry it is a single point in space from which all other figures originate. I Am is His Name and God is worthy of a capital I. Breaking this commandment is a sin against God alone.

Summary: Decalogue Dynamite

Thus there are three sins against God, one for each of the Persons of the Trinity (Commandments I, II, and III). Count these on your fingers and thumbs as Right Thumb = I, Index = II, Long = III ("the finger"). (Remember, Hebrew reads and counts from right to left.) These are summarized in the Great Commandment quotes in Mark 12:30 and Matthew 22:36 *"Thou shalt love the Lord thy God with all thy heart, with all thy soul, with all thy mind..."* Next there are three sins against society at large, or *"thy neighbor"* in the gospel quotes above *"...and the second is like unto it...".* Forgetting Sabbath, Dishonoring Parents, and Murder blend from sin against God and society to sin against a man and society (Commandments IV, V, and VI or as Right Ring = IV, Right Little = V and Left little finger = VI). Then there are three thefts against individuals: These three begin with Adultery as a sin against another person along with the rest of society and succeeding generations; then Steeling Personal Things which partially affects many other people; and finally the theft of a person's personal reputation by Bearing False Witness against them in court (Commandments VII = Left WEDDING RING FINGER, VIII = Left Long, and IX = Left index). The least and last sin of which all are guilty is the covet fuse that ignites the rest (Commandment X = Left thumb).

By associating each of the first ten letters of the Hebrew Aleph-Bet with the first ten Arabic numerals, your thumbs and fingers held out in supplication and surrender, the elements of the Periodic Table and the Ten Commandments, they will all become not only a part of your permanent memory but also a useful and productive part of your heart.

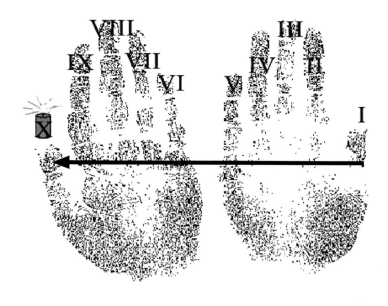

Figure 7: Hand prints of a convicted murderer (not mine)

Chapter 4

In the Beginning: ב ר א שׁ י ת

The Creation Account from Right to Left

א ל ה ה י ם א ת ה שׁ מ י ם ו א ת ה א ר ץ
ב ר א שׁ י ת ב ר א

"BARISHEET bara **Elohim** et ha'shamayim v'et **ha'aretz**"

Genesis 1

1. In the BEGINNING God created the Heavens and the **earth**
   TIME   Space   **matter**

In this foundation verse of the Word of God, the BEGINNING, as the invention of TIME, the Heavens as the invention and definition of three-dimensional Space, and the **earth** as all **Matter**, are all presented in the necessary logical order. For Time's arrow must have provided an initial reference trail on which the three dimensions of Space could grow the stage wherein the Matter of the cosmos then appeared as the creation unfolded. Matter cannot be described at all in the absence of a Time during which it may exist and a Space for it to occupy.

TIME

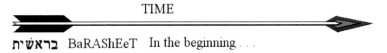

בראשית BaRAShEeT   In the beginning . . .

It is not possible that these high truths and difficult concepts were accidentally scrawled in the scientifically correct, logical, order by barely literate wandering desert nomads as they "developed their own mythology." Even with all the wisdom of the Egyptians, Moses could not have learned this scientifically accurate cosmology so eloquently stated in the first line of Genesis, even though he transcribed it. These are the very words of The Holy One who created the TSM, (Time-Space-Mass continuum).

As His very first creative act, the invisible, eternal, Spirit of the Living God thought the very notion of Time into existence as recorded by the first word in the Bible (Heb. ת י שׁ א ר ב=Ba **R A SH EE T** = "In *the* beginning"). Then, as this Hebrew word-picture records, He revealed the bodily Mass form of Himself required to interface with us as His physical creation. This aspect of the Godhead mediated between His eternal, spiritual nature (א ל ה י ם Elohim) outside of Time and the physical creation of Space (Heavens) and Matter (Earth) in which we are confined and by which we are defined. The creative act out of nothing, *ex nihlo* (Heb. א ר ב BaRA = "created") was executed from the abstractness of the immaterial eternal spiritual realm and expressed into physical existence via the medium of the spoken Word of God displayed as the Aleph-Tav ת א (or Alpha & Omega).

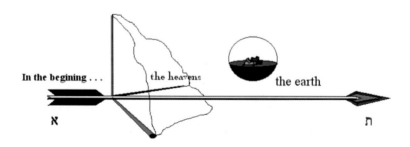

This process of speaking all things into existence may be thought of much like the numerical codes that are stored in the graphics program of a computer. The binary electronic codes dictate, number by number, the "yes's" or "no's" that will determine precisely what the three-dimensional structure will be of a complete automobile or merely an airplane engine part long before their physical reality is expressed into physical metallic form. The abstract, immaterial, magnetically recorded numbers of the computer's electronic memory occupy no space and have no mass. This information generates a three-dimensional graphic depiction on the screen that may be thought of as the intelligible language for humans of the abstract digital data. This graphic, like the words on the pages of a Bible, may then be reduced to metallic reality, in three dimensions by a computer-controlled milling machine, or through the careful reproduction of the printed schematic by a machinist. "In the beginning" of virtually anything is indeed "the word"; whether that thing be a car part, a house, a state law, The Torah, any social order or even the very Cosmos itself.

The uni-pleural proper masculine noun "Elohim" (א ל ה י ם) appears next as the third word of the Bible not by accident but to underscore that He is of three persons that is about to speak the cosmos into being as One God. This unified nature is indicated by the singular form of the verb ב ר א Bara, "Created."

$$\Omega \, \daleth \; = \; \aleph \, A$$

The very next word is made of two Hebrew letters that are peculiar. Their peculiarity and resistance to translation into any equivalent English word was the original inspiration for my inquiry into the Hebrew language in the first place. What did the lexicons and dictionaries and all the greatest minds of the ages mean when they failed to translate a simple two-letter word into

English? But the middle word of the first seven in the Bible does not easily translate into proper English. Its backwoods equivalent would be "that there" when pointing to something. This is a part of speech not common to formal English called a particle. A "particle" acts as a pointer here as in hundreds of other passages in the rest of Scripture. That central word in the first verse of the creation account is composed of only two letters. They are the letters **Aleph, א** and **Tav, ת** the **first** and the **last** letters of the Hebrew Aleph-Bet. These letters have been said by the Jewish sages, such as Moses Maimonides (1135–1204), Rabbi Moshe Ben Maimon (Rambam), to represent the whole Law or the Torah, the first five books of Moses, or the Pentateuch. But they symbolize a great deal more than just the traditions of the Mosaic Law. They encompass all twenty-two letters of the Hebrew Aleph-Bet and as such contain the potential for the entire language…every possible word. The Aleph-Tav, ת א is thought to be a contraction of ת ו א the Hebrew word OTH that means "sign, constellation, star or banner". A symbol standing for something else, therefore an ensign, like the banners for each of the 12 tribes in Numbers 2:2 or the signs in the heavens (ת ת א Genesis 1:14). But this contraction into only the two bookend letters of the Aleph-Bet symbolizes the spoken Word of God, in the beginning with God, the same as God. Ultimately the Aleph-Tav ת א indicates the Only begotten of the Father, the interface between the Eternal and the finite, the Mediator between Heaven and Earth. This simple particle stands in as a symbol for the Way God created us and our cosmos, out of nothing. The ת א Aleph-Tav "Word" is the Lord Jesus who's Greek synonym is the **Alpha** & **Omega** of Revelation **1:11**[23]. A + Ω

And just what is the first thing spoken into existence? It is the Heaven(s) (Heb. ם י מ ש ה Ha'ShAMaYiM) or the Fatherly,

---

23   Note the three 1's together in the verse notation also standing in for the **Trinity**. Revelation **1:11**

three legal dimensions of invisible Space. Those three dimensions are height, width, and depth. They cannot exist without the other, are invisible concepts, and define the physical just as the Father was revealed in His Son Jesus. The next thing spoken into the three-dimensional framework of the Heavens is the Earth, or Matter, (Heb. ץ ר א ה Ha'AReTz). Bridging these two words is the conjunction "and" (Heb. ת א ו , VAT) composed of the first letter, Aleph א , the last letter, Tav ת , coupled with the sixth letter of the Hebrew alphabet, Vav ו . This sixth letter preceding the Aleph-Tav particle "Word" lends tremendous significance to these Alpha-Omega, Beginning-and-Ending, First-and-Last, Messianic letters. For the most ancient form of this sixth letter appears as a stick with a squiggle like a snake on the top and on later Phoenician period inscriptions takes on the form of a reversed " F" or a shepherd's crook with a cross bar on it from which we get our own sixth letter in English, "f".

BETWEEN HEAVEN & EARTH

𐤅𐤉 Ancient forms of Vav

Tav ת א **Aleph**

Revelation 1:8 THE ALPHA & OMEGA *Revelation 22:13*

Isaiah 41:44 THE FIRST AND THE LAST *Isaiah 44:6*

I. Corinthians 15:22 THE LAST ADAM *I. Corinthians 15:45*

א ל ה י ם א ת ה ש מ י ם ו א ת ה א ר ץ
ב ר א ש י ת ב ר א

"Barasheet bara Elohim et ha'shamayim v'et ha'aretz"

In the beginning created God (**particle**) the heavens and the earth.

This verse may be paraphrased in many ways as follows:

In the beginning created God (<u>**1st letter & Last letter**</u>) the heavens <u>6th letter,</u> 1st letter & Last letter the earth.

In the beginning created God (by the **<u>Alpha & Omega</u>**) the heavens **<u>Alpha & Omega Man</u>**, between the earth.

In the beginning created God by the Alphabet the heavens AND the earth.

In the beginning created God via THE WORD the heavens and (a bridging conjunction) the earth.
In the beginning created God through Jesus THE WORD the heavens *with a* MEDIATOR between the earth.

John 1

1 *In the beginning* (Barasheet בּ ר א שׁ י ת) *was the Word* (Aleph-Tav א ת), *and the Word was with God* (Elohim א ל ה י ם) *and the Word was God.*

2 *The same was in the beginning with God.*

3 *All things* (Heavens & Earth ה שׁ מ י ם ו א ת ה א ר ץ) *were made by him; and without him was not any thing made that was made.*

4 *In him was life and the life was the light of men.*

5 *And the light shineth in darkness; and the darkness comprehended it not.*

I Timothy 2

5 *For there is one God* (Elohim א ל ה י ם) *and one mediator* (**Vav-Aleph-Tav = Man-WORD** ו א ת) *between God* (in Heaven ה שׁ מ י ם) *and* ו א ת *men* (on Earth ה א ר ץ), *the man Christ Jesus. Who gave himself a ransom for all, to be <u>testified</u>* [offered as **<u>Evidence</u>**] *in due time.*

In the Image of God

God created us in His image and commanded us not to make unto ourselves any graven images that would substitute for the original, Him. This has had natural consequences in both language and biology. Most of the world writes from left to right but the Word of God was written from right to left in the Old Testament. The fulfillment of the image of the Old Testament in Jesus the Messiah was documented from left to right when God became flesh and assumed the body of a man in his own image. The Testaments are symmetrical. Even the Greek New Testament if read from right to left in Semitic style has 22 epistles or letters like the Hebrew Aleph-Bet, beginning with Revelation on the far right and ending with Romans to the left. Then there are five final books that are not "letters" (epistles) like the five final forms of the Hebrew letters. These five New Testament books are Acts and the four Gospels.

This symmetry between heaven and earth is seen in the natural world of biology where vertebrates and even some invertebrates like starfish exhibit right hand and left hand symmetry, each side mirroring its opposite side. Nearly every biologically active molecule from the humble dextrose all the way up through amino acids to the information Czar DNA can exist in nature in both right handed and left handed forms called isomers. It is interesting that only one hand of the isomers is ever biologically active or useful. Right-handed dextrose is digestible sugar but its sinister mirror twin, levose, is not. The famous double helix of DNA spirals to the right because only the right-handed nucleic acids are biologically active. God created these mirror images as a parable and as a proof of his ultimate authority as the Creator.

This mirror image biochemistry means that only half of the available amino acids, purines, nucleic acids, and sugars are of any biological use. The other half of these chemicals floating around in the oceans or even the hypothetical primordial soup of Dr. Stanley Miller's 1953[24] contrived synthesis of proteins are not only useless but get in the way and stop the formation of biologically active structures. Nothing happens by chance in the works of God in nature or in the Word of God.

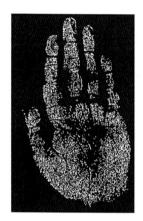 

---

24   My own naturally occurring God-designed protein synthesis went rather well the year before Stanley's experiment, culminating in the body I have been occupying ever since my own first birthday May 10, 1952.

Chapter 5

Reading Between the Lines

א ב ג ד ה ו ז ח ט י כ ל מ נ ס ע פ צ ק ר ש ת

The Hidden Authorship of the Old Testament

If you read the Bible as if it were written by wandering nomadic tribes trying to develop their mythology, there will be no morals to gain, nor any buried treasures to find. If you assume that some righteous men penned some inspiration into a poetic but technically flawed book you will gain solace in the poetry and be entertained by the stories; but little of the Spirit of the Living God will enter your mind, let alone your heart. If you read the Bible as though it were written by *"holy men of God"*[25] who were moved by the Holy Spirit to record the very word of God you will do well and find an anchor for your soul. But, if you read the Bible as if it were written by just one Author, The Word of God, then you will not only anchor your soul but you will fill your spirit, and you will find buried treasure beyond your wildest dreams; and you will get to meet the Author, Jesus.

---

25   II. Peter 1:21 *For the prophecy came not in old time by the will of man: but **holy men of God** spake as they were moved by the Holy Ghost.*

In 1996 Yacov Rambsel published his book, **YESHUA, THE NAME OF JESUS REVEALED IN THE OLD TESTAMENT** in which he established the existence of a buried code within the surface text of the Old Testament. This code was found to be one in which letters that are every fourteenth or every two hundredth etc. letter apart in the surface text would form independent sensible words and phrases such as "Jesus", "Jesus is my name", "Messiah", and others in Hebrew as a hidden code buried within the surface text of the Old Testament. When the rabbinical objections were returned that "Yeshua" was also merely the Hebrew word for "salvation" and did not necessarily mean the Jesus of Nazareth, Yacov Rambsel wrote a second and much more powerful book, **HIS NAME IS JESUS**, in which the names of all the disciples, Herod, Pilate, Caesar, Galilee, etc. were found hidden in Equidistant Letter Sequence codes in the plain text of the suffering servant messianic prophecies of Isaiah 52 and 53 five hundred years before their fulfillment at Calvary.

Isaiah 52:13-53:12

13 Behold, my servant shall deal prudently, he shall be exalted and extolled, and be very high.

14 As many were astonied at thee; his visage was so marred more than any man, and his form more than the sons of men:

15 So shall he sprinkle many nations; the kings shall shut their mouths at him: for that which had not been told them shall they see; and that which they had not heard shall they consider.

Chapter 53

1 Who hath believed our report? and to whom is the arm of the LORD revealed?

2 For he shall grow up before him as a tender plant, and as a root out of a dry ground: he hath no form nor comeliness; and when we shall see him, there is no beauty that we should desire him.

3 He is despised and rejected of men; a man of sorrows, and acquainted with grief: and we hid as it were our faces from him; he was despised, and we esteemed him not.

4 Surely he hath borne our griefs, and carried our sorrows: yet we did esteem him stricken, smitten of God, and afflicted.

5 But he was wounded for our transgressions, he was bruised for our iniquities: the chastisement of our peace was upon him; and with his stripes we are healed.

6 All we like sheep have gone astray; we have turned every one to his own way; and the LORD hath laid on him the iniquity of us all.

7 He was oppressed, and he was afflicted, yet he opened not his mouth: he is brought as a lamb to the slaughter, and as a sheep before her shearers is dumb, so he openeth not his mouth.

8 He was taken from prison and from judgment: and who shall declare his generation? for he was cut off out of the land of the living: for the transgression of my people was he stricken.

9 And he made his grave with the wicked, and with the rich in his death; because he had done no violence, neither was any deceit in his mouth.

***10 Yet it pleased the LORD** to bruise him; he hath put him to grief: when thou shalt make his soul an offering for sin, he shall see his seed, he shall **prolong his days**, and the pleasure of the LORD shall prosper in his hand.*

11 He shall see of the travail of his soul, and shall be satisfied: by his knowledge shall my righteous servant justify many; for he shall bear their iniquities.

12 Therefore will I divide him a portion with the great, and he shall divide the spoil with the strong; because he hath poured out his soul unto death: and he was numbered with the transgressors; and he bare the sin of many, and made intercession for the transgressors.

י ש כ י ל ע ב ד י י ר ו ם ו נ ש א ו ג ב ה מ א ד :
13. ה נ ה

ע ל י ך ר כ י ם כ ן מ ש ח ת מ א י ש מ ר א ה ו
14. כ א ש ר ש מ מ ו

ו ת א ר ו מ ב נ י א ר ם :

ע ל י ו י ק פ צ ו מ ל כ י ם פ י ה ם כ י א ש ר
15. כ ן י ז ה ה ג ו י ם ר ב י ם

ל ה ס ר א ו ר א ש ר ל א ־ ש מ ע ו ה ת ב ו נ נ ו :
ל א ־ ס פ ר

ו ז ר ו ע י ה ו ה ע ל ־ מ י נ ג ל ת ה Chapt. 53:
1. מ י ה א מ י ן ל ש מ ע ת נ ו

ל פ נ י ו ו כ ש ר ש מ א ר ץ צ י ה ל א ־ ת א ר
2. ו י ע ל כ י ו נ ק

ה ד ר ו נ ר א ה ו ו ל א ־ מ ר א ה ו נ ח מ ד ה ו :
ל ו ו ל א

ו ח ד ל א י ש י מ א י ש מ כ א נ ו ת ו י ד ו ע
3. נ ב ז ה

פ נ י ם מ מ נ ו ו נ ב ז ה ו ל א א ח ש ב נ ה ו :
ח ל י ו כ מ ס ת ר

א כ ן ח ל י נ ו ה ו א נ ש א ו מ כ א ב י נ ו ס ב ל ם
4.

ח ש ב נ ה ו נ ג ו ע מ כ ה א ל ה י ם ו מ ע נ ה :
ו א נ ח נ ו

מ ח ל ל מ פ ש ע י נ ו מ ד כ א מ ע ו נ ת י נ ו
5. ו ה ו א

ש ל ו מ נ ו ע ל י ו ו ב ח ב ר ת ו נ ר פ א ־ ל נ ו :
מ ו ס ר

כ ל נ ו כ א ן ת ע י נ ו א י ש ל ד ר כ ו
6. פ נ י נ ו ו י ה ו ה ה פ ג י ע ב ו א ת ע ו ן כ ל נ ו :

ו ה ו א נ ע נ ה ו ל א י פ ת ח ־ פ י ו כ ש ה ל ט ב ח

7. נ ג ש

ל פ נ י ג ז י ה נ א ל מ ה ו ל א י פ ת ה פ י ו :
י ו ב ל ו כ ר ח ל

ו מ מ ש פ ט ל ק ח ו א ת ־ ד ו ר ו מ י י ש ו ח ח

8. מ ע צ ר

נ ג ז ר מ א ר ץ ח י י ם מ פ ש ע ע מ י נ ג ע ל מ ו :
כ י

־ ר ש ע י ם ק ב ר ו ו א ת ־ ע ש י ר ב מ ת י ו

9. ו י ת ן א ת

𐤔 ל ל א ־ ח מ ס ע ש ה ו ל א א מ ר מ ה ב פ י ו <u>ן</u> :
ד כ א ו ה ח ל י א ם ־ ת 𐤔 י ם א ש מ נ פ ש ו

<u>**10.** ו י ה ו ה ח פ ץ</u>

י מ י ם ו ח פ צ י י ה ו ה ב י ד ו י צ ל ח :
י ר א ה ז ר ע י א ר <u>ך</u>

נ פ ש ו י ר א ה י ש ב ע ב ד ע ת ו צ ד י ק

11. מ ע מ ל

ע ב ד י ל ר ב י ם ו ע ו נ ת מ ה ו א י ס ב ל :
צ ד י ק

־ ל ו ב ר ב י מ ו א ת ־ ע צ ו מ י ם י ח ל ק

12. ל כ ן א ח ל ק

ת ח ת א ש ר ה ע ר ה ל מ ו ת נ פ ש ו ו א ת ־
ש ל ל

ח ט א ־ ר ב י ם נ ש א ו ל פ ש ע י ם י פ ג י ע :
פ ש ע י ם נ מ נ ה ו ה ו א

In the Hebrew passage above taken from the suffering servant chapters of Isaiah, Yacov Rambsel notes the following proper names hidden within the plain text in equidistant letter sequences as reproduced in this chart:

Name	Beginning text	Word #	Letter #	Interval (skip)
Yeshua ש ו ש י confirm these yourself	Isaiah 53:10 ח פ ץ ה ו ה י י 10.	11th ר ר א י	4th **yod**	L to R - 20 (Skip every 20th letter, from Right to Left. Blue Outlined)
Nazarene נ ז ר י	Isaiah 53:6	11th	3rd	R to L +47
Messiah מ י ש m	Isaiah 53:11	1st	1st	L to R -42
Shiloh ה ל י W	Isaiah 53:12	21st	4th	R to L +19
Passover פ ס ח	Isaiah 53:10	13th	3rd	L to R -62
Galilee ל י ל g	Isaiah 53:7	1st	2nd	L to R -32
Herod א י ש ה ו ר ד	Isaiah 53:6	4th	1st	L to R -29
Caesar (wicked, perish) ק י ס ר ע מ ל א ו ד	Isaiah 53:11	7th	4th	L to R -194
The Evil Roman City ז ע ע י ר ר ו מ י	Isaiah 53:9	13th	2nd	L to R -7
Caiaphas, High Priest י פ ח k	Isaiah 53:15	7th	3rd	R to L +41
Annas, High Priest נ ן f	Isaiah 53:3	6th	5th	L to R -45
Mary מ ר י ם	Isaiah 53:11	1st	1st	L to R -23
Mary מ ר י ם	Isaiah 53:10	7th	3rd	R to L +6
Mary מ ר י ם	Isaiah 53:9	13th	3rd	R to L +44
The Disciples ל מ ד י ם	Isaiah 53:12	2nd	3rd	L to R -55
Peter כ פ ה	Isaiah 53:10	11th	5th	L to R -14
Matthew מ ת ת י	Isaiah 53:8	12th	1st	L to R -295
John י ו ח נ ן	Isaiah 53:10	11th	4th	L to R -28
Andrew א נ ד ר י	Isaiah 53:4	11th	1st	L to R -48
Philip פ י ל פ	Isaiah 53: 5	10th	3rd	L to R -133
Thomas ת ו מ א	Isaiah 53:2	8th	1st	R to L +35
James י ע ק ב	Isaiah 52:2	9th	3rd	L to R -34
James י ע ק ב	Isaiah 52:2	3rd	4th	L to R -20

Yacov Rambsel found all of these amazing hidden codes linking Jesus of Nazareth with the prophecies of the suffering Messiah by hand, without the aid of computerized mathematical programs. They are used here with his generous permission and only represent about ten percent of the Yeshua codes present in Isaiah 53. The odds of finding these Equidistant Letter Sequence Bible Codes manually are nearly as astronomical as the chance of their existence in the first place. They are noted here not only because of the wonderful fact of their revelation at this time in history to our generation, but also as the obvious witness they will provide a re-gathering Nation of Israel. These codes are mathematical proofs that the Lord Jesus Christ, this same Jesus of Nazareth, who suffered and died for us on Calvary is the prophesied Messiah of Israel. He is expected to return shortly.

Equidistant Letter Sequences and "The Bible Codes"

Yacov Rambsel's inspired revelations of the Equidistant Letter Sequences by hand were only possible under the direction of the Holy Spirit. There is yet another method of finding these codes using the modern high-speed computer as a key that unlocks one of the seals that has kept Daniel's prophetic book such a mystery "*sealed up*" until this "*time of the end*".[26]

The twenty-two consonant letters of the Hebrew Aleph-Bet may be strung together like pearls on a strand without spaces between their words or page breaks. This linear strand of the letters of the Bible may be wrapped around any hypothetical cylinder of a specified diameter and thereby produce a page of text with columns and rows adjusted to comply with the size of the cylinder. On the page as defined by the cylinder a cross-word puzzle may form with horizontal, vertical, and diagonal words appearing out of the surface text in a nearly infinite number of possible permutations. There could be literally billions of possible hidden codes within this system of letter arrangements. Any change in circumference of the mathematical cylinder of one letter or more would shift not only columns but also rows and diagonals.

---

26   Daniel 12:9 *And he* [the angel] *said, Go thy way, Daniel: for the words are closed up and sealed till the time of the end.*

<u>The Bible Code</u>, by Michael Drosnin, is a popular coffee table book that melodramatically demonstrates the consequences of this quality of the Bible that sets it apart from any other literature. Drosnin's sensational and somewhat bizarre popular writing draws on the very sound and precise scientific work of Dr. Eliyahu Rips, Dr. Doron Witzum, and Dr. Yoav Rosenberg of Hebrew University in Jerusalem. They first published their findings in the serious discipline of statistical analysis and their research remains un-refuted in the scientific mathematical literature to this day. Using the Masoretic text of Genesis taken as one long string of letters wrapped around various mathematically determined cylinders, from a tall thin cylinder on one extreme to a short fat cylinder at the other extreme, Prof. Rips and his colleagues could generate a nearly infinite variety of page combinations with columns and rows of coiled strings of scripture that depended upon the dimensions of the cylinder. This was all done mathematically of course, but the

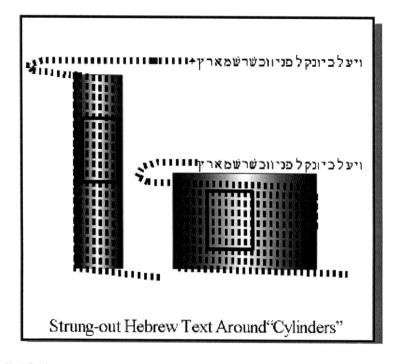

Strung-out Hebrew Text Around "Cylinders"

result was a computer program that could find the hidden ELS-s, or Equidistant Letter Sequences in vertical, horizontal and diagonal rows. It was discovered that, for at least the book of Genesis, the names of sixty six of the greatest Medieval Jewish Sages (all born after the final Masoretic text of the Bible was established only about a thousand years ago) could be entered into the computer program and their birth and death dates would be found on the same page in some pattern of ELS associated with that name. That's right, for every single one, and with perfect accuracy.

It is, of course, impossible that such an association should or could occur by chance or even with some extraordinary human thought and planning, but this remarkable pattern of associations does in fact appear with an incredible regularity. There are so many hidden names, dates, and specific information contained in the Bible that their presence impelled Mr. Drosnin to his illogical and silly conclusion that the Torah was given by time-traveling space aliens to Moses through a computer called "The Ark of the Covenant"! Mr. Drosnin was forced to conclude such a ridiculous thing because the only other alternative is that the Word of God is, in fact, exactly what it claims to be, "*quick* or **living** *and powerful*". The Genius of Vilna in Lithuania once said that everything that ever would be was already contained in the Torah. As it turns out he was right. The Hebrew text of Torah contains every possible event down to the smallest detail throughout history embedded deep within the latticework of its surface literary text. Even a single letter transposition or omission would shift the string of letters along so that the code would fail. Yet the Bible Code works; not with the Syriac text; nor the original autograph (which has never been located); nor with any other than the Masoretic text. That text was not really finalized until about 800 AD. The text that works in this code must be alive. "*For the word of God is quick (alive) and powerful. . .*" Hebrews 4:12 and self preserving much like another code designed by God, such as the genetic code and DNA both mentioned in Psalm 139:14 & 15. The next chapter takes us into the basis of all life where we will see that DNA may also contain Bible codes.

Chapter 6

DNA: The Smallest TLA (Three Letter Acronym)

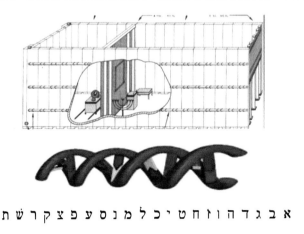

א ב ג ד ה ו ז ח ט י כ ל מ נ ס ע פ צ ק ר ש ת

More 3 Letter Codes
DNA and The Amino Acid Alphabet of Life

In the late 1940's just after the Nation of Israel had returned to the world scene and the Dead Sea Scrolls were found, another incredible code was discovered. DNA, Deoxy-ribo-Nucleic Acid, the famous and now infamous, double helix ladder of life, was being researched by Watson and Crick. By the time the last 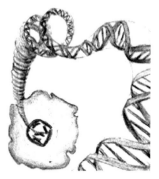 major Dead Sea cave was cleared of its precious treasure of encoded scrolls in 1952 the detailed structure of DNA's spiraling base pairs of nucleic acids had been published. This was just in time for my own DNA to finally express itself into a physical body for me to use by May 10, 1952. My blue eyes and straight brown-black hair, freckles, Norman nose, and knuckle-dragging long arms, were already programmed by the genetic DNA of twenty-two pairs of chromosomes plus the X and Y sex chromosomes. All of this genetic information was encoded nine months earlier in my mother's womb. The codes that described me were tucked away in long spiral strands of DNA that coiled up into the nucleus of a cell not as big as the period at the end of this sentence.

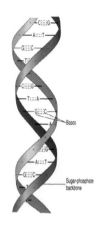

Watson and Crick, working in their laboratory far away outside my mother's womb, discovered that the entire genetic blueprint for all living things was determined by the pairing and orderly sequence of only four fairly simple nucleic acids, Thymine, Adenine, Cytosine and Guanine. They were called nucleic acids because they were first extracted from the nucleus of the cell. But the code was even simpler that the four nucleic acids because the acids always occurred in pairs. Thymine always paired with Adenine to make a ladder rung of the double helix spiral ladder. Cytosine always paired with Guanine to make the other version of a ladder rung. This made only two base pair ladder rung types T-A and C-G. These rungs with different ends could produce only four possible combinations; T-A, A-T, C-G, & G-C. This elegantly simple plan made it possible to encode the blueprint for trillions of molecules in each of trillions of cells in each of trillions of organs in each of trillions of carbon-based life forms. These two simple types of ladder rungs that joined

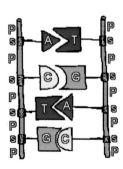

the spiraling rails of the double stranded DNA were found to occur in triplets. These triplets were found to be unique codes for each of 22 amino acids, the building blocks of proteins that form all biological tissues and hormones. For example; the sequence [T-A, A-T, G-C] is TAG on one of the spiral strands that codes for the amino-acid building block molecule Isoleucine. Each of the 22 amino acids of a structural protein could be coded by a triplet of nucleic acids aligned on the spiral strands of DNA. (Check it out for yourself in Appendix V.)

Over the next thirty years of research in many other laboratories it was determined that the DNA hidden in the nucleus of the cell is never directly translated into proteins. Rather transfer and messenger nucleic acid chains act as copies in the millions out in the cell to make the proteins. Transfer and Messenger RNA like DNA act as template jigs for the assembly of the building block amino acids into all of the myriad of proteins that define what the living world of plants and animals, people and germs, bugs and parasites all look like.

By this ingenious code of only three nucleic acids for each of 22 amino acids, protein and polypeptide strands snap into their unique shapes based on their acid base and electrical properties. Flat sheets of protein chains form skin while long thin strands form hair and fiber and cubical solid shapes help form the hard matrix of bones. All biological life on earth is determined by this most fundamental of all codes. Appendix V lists the entire DNA to RNA to Amino Acid codes.

Moses Tabernacle: A Model of the Biological Cell

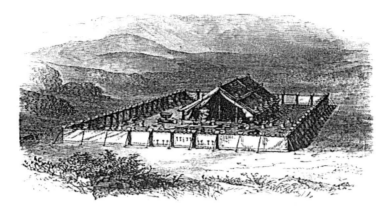

In the Tabernacle that Moses set up in the wilderness the original stone tables inscribed with the Decalogue, and the five Books of The Torah were sealed inside the Ark of the Covenant (the "chromosome" box) in the perfectly cubical Holy of Holies (the "nucleus" of the Tabernacle "cell"). Only once each year on Yom Kippur was the High Priest permitted to enter this inner sanctum. Any unauthorized entry any other time for anyone else was fatal. So access to the original copies of the scripture was very limited. Copies of this original hidden Pentateuch were maintained outside the veil in the Holy Place. This was an adjacent room to the forbidden Holy of Holies yet still within the tent covering of the Tabernacle. Within the Holy Place Levites would make interpretations of those scriptures, transferring excerpts and whole chapters into many copies. These accessible copies of the sacred Scriptures were then sent by messengers to be applied to certain judicial and social problems as they came up among the masses of the people in the camp outside the courtyard of the Tabernacle.

This is of course a picture of the tightly coiled DNA hidden in the strands of chromatin in the chromosomes of the nucleus of any eukaryotic cell. Only some of the official copy of the DNA is ever expressed via Transfer RNA and Messenger RNA into proteins outside of the nucleus by the masses in the cytoplasm, much like how the original Torah books written by Moses were hidden away in the Ark of the Covenant. Only parts of that Torah were copied out and distributed to the camp outside the Tabernacle courtyard.

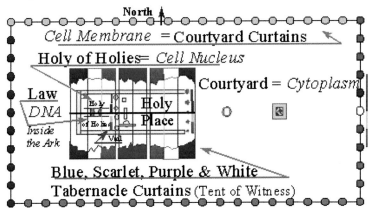

When amino acid letters are strung together and ordered into long strands or sentences by their nucleic acid codons they spell out small words as polypeptides such as insulin or vasopressin or digestive enzymes. They may spell out very long words or phrases (proteins) such as those that make up complex enzymes, muscle fibers, liver cell organelles etc. Yet it is all controlled by three letter codons of nucleic acids in the nucleus and is finally expressed by twenty-two amino acids strung out like letters that form words, phrases and sentences. The DNA code for each of these body proteins may even be seen in Psalm 139:13-16 where the phrase, "*in **thy book** all my members **were written** when as yet there was none of them*" clearly indicates a genetic code like DNA.

The Amino Acids
Building Blocks of Life[27]
The Alphabet of Polypeptide Words & Protein Sentences

1. Alanine, Ala A

2. Arginine, Arg R

3. Asparagine, Asn N

4. Aspartic acid, Asp D

5. Cysteine, Cys C

6. Glutamic acid, Glu E

7. Glutamine, Gln Q

8. Glycine, Gly G

9. Histidine, His H

10. Isoleucine, Ile I

11. Leucine, Leu L

12. Lysine, Lys K

13. Methionine, Met M

14. Phenylalanine, Phe F

15. Proline, Pro P

16. Serine, Ser S

17. Threonine, Thr T

18. Tryptophan, Trp W

19. Tyrosine, Tyr Y

20. Valine, Val V

21. Hydroxy Proline, (Structural component of cartilage)

22. Gamma Amino Butyric Acid, (GABA), a neurotransmitter

---

27   According to Dorland's Medical Dictionary there are more than thirty amino acids twenty-one of which are most commonly found in protein structures. The 22nd amino acid listed here as GABA could have been any of about a dozen other rarely encountered structural amino acids found in nature besides the 21 basic building block acids.

Isn't it an odd coincidence that the number of naturally occurring amino acids that make up the twenty-two or so letters of every polypeptide "word" or the proteins of biological "sentences" match the same number as the twenty-two letters of the Hebrew language of The Book? The language our Creator used to communicate His wisdom to us matches the pattern of the language structure of all life. Why are there three nucleic acids (a government by a Trinity) per DNA codon at the highest level of control? Why not four base pairs or two or seven? There is a scientific and theological Trinity that extends out into the mega-dimensions of the cosmos of Time-Space-Matter or down into atomic protons, neutrons and electrons or even into the sub-atomic Up, Down, and Neutral particles of quantum mechanics. The Trinity and absolutes of the Godhead permeate His Universe in threes and are expressed into our lives in twenty-two amino acids of the Works of God and twenty-two letters of the Hebrew Aleph-Bet in the Word of God.

The genetic code is written in very simple nucleic acid sequences that translate into a more complex alphabet of many more amino acids and then out into millions of proteins and all biological life forms. If this natural biological code in the physical realm could be hidden in the very simple letters of a few organic chemicals why does it seem strange to some people that there could be a similar code of all events in history embedded in the surface text of the Bible? If there are secret codes embedded in DNA and proteins and there are secret codes hidden in the Hebrew letter sequences of the Bible, could there be a relationship between them? What if each of the amino acids corresponded to a letter of the Hebrew Aleph-Bet? Could we have a head start in the Human Genome Project with protein amino acid sequences laid out in plain sight in the pages of the Torah? Could the very Word of God be written in the amino acid sequences of all nature? Do both heav'n and nature sing joy to the world far more literally than the Christmas carol composer ever dreamt?

There is another encrypted message in nature and Scripture that is revealed in the dots on ii's and j's. This ij code impressed even on the landscape of Jerusalem deals with eternity and practical daily life in the next chapter.

"i, jesus"

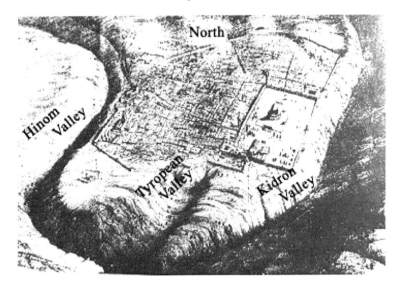

א ב ג ד ה ה ו ז ח ט י כ ל מ נ ס ע פ צ ק ר ש ת

י ד שׁ ל א , **El Shaddai**

The Protector

Jerusalem rests on the summit of Mount Moriah from which three steep valleys converge together down its south face. These topographical maps of Jerusalem depict that trinity of valleys (in solid lines) as they would appear from above. These valleys appear to form the three branches of the Letter Shin שׁ or Sin שׂ (depending on where the dot is placed).

To the southwest (on the left) is the Hinom Valley where Canaanite children were sacrificed to the pagan god, Molech. This is also where the Aceldama, or Potter's Field, of Judas Iscariot's blood money was located. This valley was also called "Gehenna" or "Hell" because it smoldered with burning trash all the time. It was to this valley that Jesus pointed from the Temple Portico as he told the parable of Lazarus and the Rich Man because this valley also separated the rich Hasmonean ruling class from the paupers.

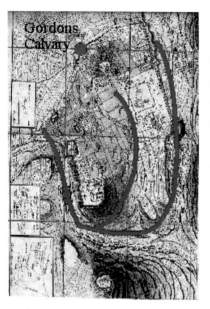

The middle valley is the Tyropean Valley, or Valley of the Cheese (makers?) possibly named for its steepness as a cheese-wedge-shaped valley in cross-section. The Western Wall or the Wailing Wall forms part of its eastern slope as the western retaining wall of the Temple Mount. This steep cleft still divides modern Mount Zion into two parts that have become known in recent times as the Temple Mount to the east and Mount Zion to the west. But, in Bible times both hills were called "Zion" and make up the slope of Mount Moriah, where Abraham offered up his son, Isaac.

The Kidron Valley, better known as the Valley of Jehoshaphat (Heb. *Jah [God] is Judge* ט פ שׁ ו ה י), is located farthest east (on the right) and marks the division between Mount Moriah and the Mount of Olives. This is the traditional site of the Last Judgment and is lined on both slopes with the graveyards of those over the millennia who have wanted to reserve the best seats for this coming event.

Gordon's Calvary, also known as the Garden Tomb, is indicated by the large dot on the very summit of Mount Moriah. The confluence of all three valleys forms the outline of the Hebrew letter Shin שׁ , or Sin שׂ, depending on the location of the dot.

Shin שׁ is the first letter of one of the names of God in the Bible.

אֵל שַׁדַּי , El Shaddai is the name of God that signifies His almighty power and protection. The word "שַׁדַּי , Shaddai" comes from the root for "breast" שַׁד "Shad" as in a nurturing, provider-protector God. This Divine protection of Jerusalem has been demonstrated throughout history, even the history of its many invasions and sieges. Jerusalem has been taken by force, overthrown, or destroyed dozens of times in its three thousand year history. The old college football cheer, *"**Hep, Hep, Hurrah**"* is a reminder to us from Roman times of just how hated the people of God and Jerusalem have been. **"HEP"** stands for the Latin, **H**erusalem **E**st **P**ereo, "Jerusalem Is Perished". Jerusalem has been taken from the north by pagan invaders every time. In fact only twice has it been conquered from the south. Jeremiah 1:13 points out this illegitimate invasion from the north; " . . . *Out of the north an evil shall break forth upon all the inhabitants of the land.*" Ezekiel prophesied that it would be Gog and Magog out of the north that will assemble on the plains of Jezreel to the north of Jerusalem at the base of the Megiddo Tell called "Har Megiddo". Ezekiel predicted that they would attack Jerusalem from the north in the final conflict, [H]Ar-mageddon.

Ezekiel Chapter 38

[14] *Therefore, son of man, prophesy and say unto Gog, Thus saith the Lord GOD; In that day when my people of Israel dwelleth safely, shalt thou not know it?*

[15] *And thou shalt come from thy place **out of the north parts**, thou, and many people with thee, all of them riding upon horses, a great company, and a mighty army:*

The shallow grade at the northern summit of Jerusalem's Mount Moriah has always been the path of least resistance for every invading general from Babylonian King Nebuchadnezzar and Roman General Titus in the ancient world to Geoffrey and the

Crusaders or even British General Edmund Allenby during World War I. Yet only twice in history the city was taken through the steep valleys and sheer rock faces of its divinely protected southern walls.

The first time was when King David took the city by having Joab shinny up the southern fissure-waterway into what eventually became known as the Pool of Siloam. The second conquest of Jerusalem through its protective southern walls came when Israeli Colonel Mordekhai Gur attacked through the Lion's Gate, and by 10:15 A.M. took the city on June 7, 1967 during the Six-Day War.

Legitimate invited citizens of Jerusalem have never invaded her from the north, but have been invited through El Shaddai's protective breastworks of the southern walls.

The Messiah will enter into His gates with praise from the Eastern or Golden Gate just as every Israelite did at the one and only Eastern Gate of the Wilderness Tabernacle that Moses erected at the foot of Jabal Al Lawz in Midian (Arabia) due south of Jerusalem. The tribe that Jesus, The Messiah, came from was Judah, which meant "Praise". Judah encamped around the entrance to the Eastern Gate of the Wilderness Tabernacle before the Temple was built at Jerusalem, and those who entered that gate with sin offerings, sacrifices, and all their guilt, entered into his gates with praise as they walked through singing Judah (the tribe out of whom would come the Messiah) to get to the gate. The compass direction we take and the gate we choose to enter life's problems matter as much today as they always have in the past in the wilderness wanderings, in the Land of Israel, at Jerusalem, or in the uttermost parts of the earth.

One other evil rebellion took place in the north when Satan defied God;

Isaiah 14

*13 For thou hast said in thine heart, I will ascend into heaven, I will exalt my throne above the stars of God: I will sit also upon the mount of the congregation, **in the sides of the north**:*

Unto this day the most northern constellation in the heavens is Draco the Dragon, that Old Serpent, the Devil.

In 1883 British General "Chinese" Charles Gordon went to Jerusalem in search of a figurative skeleton he had deciphered from the Hebrew text of Jeremiah. According to his reckoning the skull of that rocky figure of a skeleton would have been north of the city. While enjoying a sunset one evening on the roof of Horatio Spafford's[28] house on the wall between Herod's Gate and the Damascus Gate, General Gordon spotted a distinct skull-like rock feature. He and millions of others since then have come to the conclusion that this could have been the Place of the Skull, "Golgotha" in Hebrew, "Calvary", in Latin.

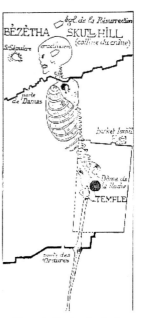

Figure 9. Charles Gordon's Drawing of Golgotha

---

28   Horatio Gates Spafford was a professor of medical jurisprudence from Chicago who maintained a close friendship with D. L. Moody and other Christian leaders. He was the author of the hymn, "**It Is Well With My Soul**" written after the loss of four daughters at sea November 22, 1873. He and his wife moved to Jerusalem when he was 60 to establish the American Colony where Gen. Gordon saw the skull in 1883.

Jesus on the Cross, facing South

Garden Tomb to Jesus' right
(West)

Golgotha, Skull Hill to Jesus' left (East)

All of this is evidence that the Lord Jesus Christ was probably crucified north of the city of Jerusalem on the summit of Mount Moriah. To the east on this south-facing escarpment is the unmistakable image of a skull face. The garden tomb is cut into the western face of the Calvary Escarpment. Skull Hill and the

garden tomb are within a few hundred yards of each other on the same south facing cliff face. On either side of the tomb entrance are niches cut into the rock face that held signs declaring the occupants of the tomb. There are also three cutouts in the rock face of the Calvary Escarpment midway

Figure 10. Niche Cut-out east of the tomb door is similar to three others around the Skull Face to the east

between the face of the skull and the tomb. These niches would have held signs as large as two feet high and four feet wide to proclaim the crimes of those being crucified beneath them. One of these signs read *JESUS OF NAZARETH, KING OF THE JEWS* in Latin, Greek, and Aramaic (Hebrew).

If the Lord Jesus truly were crucified at or near Gordon's Calvary (the dot north of Jerusalem on the topographical map) he would have been facing the busy traffic of the highway to the south of the Calvary Escarpment as an example for all of those passing by of the truly brutal Pax Romana "justice". His bruised and bleeding back would have been to the north with the weight of the whole world's Sin upon those stripes. Placed by the Romans in this position (without his consent, manipulation, or suggestion) the Lord Jesus would have fulfilled the prophetic statements he had made to Satan and Peter many months earlier.

Matthew 16

²³ *But he turned, and said unto Peter,* **Get thee behind me, Satan**:[**Draco the Dragon in the northern sky**] *thou art an offence unto me: for thou savourest not the things that be of God, but those that be of men.*

²⁴ *Then said Jesus unto his disciples, If any man will come after me, let him deny himself, and* **take up his cross**, *and follow me.*

Luke 4

8 *And Jesus answered and said unto him,*[the Devil] **Get thee behind me, Satan**: *for it is written, Thou shalt worship the Lord thy God, and him only shalt thou serve.*

The Lord's back would have been toward the northern constellation of the Dragon.

The Lord Jesus would also have been offering Himself as the ultimate sacrifice with His blood sprinkled north of the altar of Herod's temple, and precisely due north of Moses' first Tabernacle erected at the base of Mount Sinai in Arabia.

Leviticus 1:11

[11] ***And he shall kill it on the side of the altar <u>northward</u>** before the LORD: and the priests, Aaron's sons, shall sprinkle his blood round about upon the altar.*

Much more could be said about the special and geographical relationships of the Crucifixion than we are able to digest in this little work. For now it is important to note that the site of Gordon's Calvary dovetails with both the factual descriptions of Scripture and the prophetic symbolism those facts are meant to convey to us. That location of Calvary also changes the pronunciation of the Hebrew letter "Shin" שׁ to "SIN" שׂ in our illustration of the providence of God protecting the southern breastworks of Jerusalem. For the Lord Jesus was made sin for us at Calvary and the Garden Tomb makes a real point even in translation into English semantics. Points are important. Even the dots on the i's and j's or the crosses on the t's and f's are important clues into our salvation.

Why Are i's and j's Dotted?

Besides remembering our p's and q's we all have a very old basic command placed in our minds by some elementary school teacher years ago to dot our "i"s and cross our "t"s. Why are there dotted letters and crossed letters in the English alphabet that require such diligence from little school children? It may be that when the Lord God invented language He implanted some of His thoughts even at the root of all languages in their letters. It would be in His divine nature, much the same as the genes and DNA reflect His Triune nature; for there are four letters in English i, j, f and t that need servicing with added marks. I and J are really the same letter in Latin and other languages leaving us with the Trinity of letters that have added markings; i&j, t & f.

I and J are the ninth and tenth letters of the English Alphabet and are somewhat synonymous with Y also. All three have only one equivalent in the Hebrew Aleph-bet in the form of a Yod י , the first letter of Jehovah, ה ו ה י Jesus (Yeshua) ע ו ש י , and the tenth letter in Hebrew. The Tenth Commandment is "Thou shalt not covet" and, as we have seen, acts as the silent internal fuse of desire that can light off all the other nine more and more offensive commandments. If we list the Ten Commandments in reverse order from top to bottom as Ten through One, we have constructed a figure of a stick of dynamite with the Tenth Covet Commandment as a little fuse stuck on the top of the body of the column of overt commandments. That same figure also resembles the lower case i, and looks like a little man with the dot as his head. Think of i as a symbol for fallen mankind with a big body ego and a limited mind on the top. As the ninth letter mankind's little i symbol is living under judgment and subject to the curse of Adam with a penalty of death hanging over his nearly severed head all the time.

Even as in Adam all die, so in Christ shall all be made alive. The name of Jesus (Yeshua) ה ו ש י begins with the tenth letter of the English alphabet, j, which also has a mind dotting its "j" shaped body. Yeshua means "Salvation" and it is the curse of Adam, the judgment and death that we i's are saved from in Jesus. Ten is the number of ordinal perfection and renewal in Scripture and so symbolizes our new life "in Jesus".

Imagine the helpless little i supported on the up curving limb of the salvation "j". This forms a "U" with a dot on each upright limb in a person in union with Christ. "U" then have two minds; your "old man" i-dot and your new creature in Christ Jesus j-dot that are always at odds on opposite sides of every issue "U" face. Whenever there is disagreement between the i-dot mind and j-dot mind, remember that it is the up curving limb of the "j" that is supporting all of the old man i. "*i am crucified with Christ: nevertheless i live; yet not i but Christ liveth in me: and the life which IJ now live in the flesh IJ live by the faith of the Son of God, who loved me and gave Himself for me.*" Galatians 2:20

Let's take a look at one last English word from Latin; "crucifixion". Note that the central letter is an "f". It is a cross and shepherd's crook shaped upright letter. "f" is the sixth letter of the English alphabet and as the sixth letter it stands for the number of man. It is also in the sixth position from either end of the word "crucifixion". i am crucified on either side of this shepherd-man letter. There are three i's in the word crucifixion, one for each of the Trinity, for Jesus The Son could not have been separated from The Holy Spirit or The Father in His payment for our sin at Calvary. There is yet one more curiosity about the cross that is present in this very wonderful word. The "**X**" which is the first letter if the word in Greek for **Ch**rist, Χριστοσ, is a cross-shaped letter and i am also crucified on either side of that symbol for Messiah, the Anointed One. Whenever someone tries to remove the Christ from Christmas by abbreviating it as X-mass they are really advertising the Cross. At Christmas we celebrate the incarnation of God Himself into the world who gave Himself for U and i on an X-shaped cross that the shepherd's crook f and the t commemorate. The last letter of the Hebrew Aleph-Bet is Tav ת . This letter was written in ancient Phoenician Hebrew as the cross-shaped t it eventually became in English.

I hope you have enjoyed this whirlwind tour of the basic Hebrew letters. If you have lost your fear of these ancient letters then the most basic objective of this book has occurred in your mind. If you have made friends with these letters and gained a familiarity with them in order to comprehend an interlinear Hebrew Bible or a concordance then you have gained a practical study skill. If you have grown in your relationship with your Creator and Savior on His terms in His own words then you have received a priceless gift that can never be taken from you.

If you would, please return to the Prologue and read it as the Epilogue for which it was first composed. It will seal the message of this book in your heart.

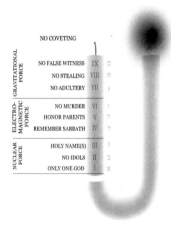

Author's Note (Pocket Edition)

This book had humble beginnings as a footnote in an appendix at the back of a fiction work called **Ralph and The Sons of God**. I wanted to describe in graphic detail what the world before the Great Flood of Noah must have been like. In the process of researching the biblical and secular evidence left from the antediluvian world, I discovered that more than just the material fossils of dinosaurs were buried in the waters of Noah's Flood. I also found remnants from the pre-flood world of what I called "fossils of Time" and "fossils of Space". These "fossils" are buried in layers of myths, sagas, and legends in every culture on earth. I appended a factual chapter on this trinity of Time, Space, and Matter to the fictional novel. That humble appendix later grew into an independent book called **The Fossils of Time Space and Matter.** These "fossils" of Time, Space, and Matter seemed to correspond to an interesting biblical perspective on the trinity of time-space-matter first put forth by Dr. Henry Morris in his 1976 book **THE GENESIS RECORD**.

Dr. Morris had noted that Genesis 1:1 recorded this Time-Space-Matter continuum in the only scientifically logical order as "*In the beginning* (Time) *God created the heavens* (Space) *and the earth* (Matter)." This pattern became even more obvious in the original Hebrew where I noticed that one little word made a world of difference. That tiny fourth word of the Bible had no English equivalent translation. It was the particle word "*et*", ת א or the Aleph-Tav, the first and last letters of the Hebrew Aleph-Bet, the Hebrew equivalent of the Greek in Revelation "*The Alpha and Omega . . . the First and the Last . . . the Beginning and the End*". It was only two letters long but tracking it back to its Hebrew roots lead me down a rabbit hole into strange new territory of a Wonderland that even Alice would have found fascinating. Look for **THE FOSSILS OF TIME SPACE AND MATTER, RALPH AND THE**

SONS OF GOD and **FALLING STARS** coming soon. Li'l ol' **ALEPH-BET SOUP** seems to have beaten them all to the punch.

I hope that you have become friends with the fascinating characters that make up the Hebrew Aleph-Bet. But I wish above all things that you may prosper in health even as your soul (nephesh) prospers as a result of digesting the king's feast that my dear friend, Yacov Rambsel, called this little book. He and mom are now feasting together in person with Jesus the Messiah, The ת א , awaiting our reunion in eternity. Please return to the prologue now and appreciate the spirit that still resides in you as long as you draw breath. The breath of life that God breathed into you, as a descendant of Adam, is only a loan and will be recalled one day. It would be wonderful if you could dine with Yacov and Mom, and all the rest of the all-volunteer army of the Lord by simply accepting the New Birth breath of the Holy Spirit of God that will not be only on loan for a short lifetime. That Holy Breath of Life earned by Jesus at His resurrection is eternal.

Toda ה ד ו ת (thanks)

Charles J. Thurston, MD

Kingston, Ohio

Saturday, May 26, 2007

Appendix I.

NUMBER SYMBOLISM IN SCRIPTURE

The following list is not numerology nor is it intended to validate numerology's perversion of the patterns and divine order God has encoded in His Word. It is provided here as a brief summary of the scholarly work of a host of Bible students over the centuries. The numerical patterns that the Author of all things (including our salvation) embedded in His works and His Word serve to seal His promises to us.

1. ONE: UNITY, Commencement, initial direction Creation Day 1; (Time Space Mass) as one Trinity
The light released into the void of its absence
A single point in space
(Not a Prime Number)

2. TWO: DIFFERENCE, division, opposing ends, marriage Creation Day 2; firmament-divided-waters
(1ˢᵗ Prime Number),
Two points in space that define a straight line

3. THREE: TRINITY, Creative Completeness,
Creation Day 3; Earth rises up out of sea, Plants rise up out of the earth
Like the Resurrection of the Lord Jesus Christ
(2ⁿᵈ Prime Number)
3rd side of the simplest geometric plane figure; the triangle

4. FOUR: EARTH, 3+1=**4:** Creator (The Trinity) 3 + His unique Creation, = focused on **the earth**;
Ha'aretz ץ ר א ה a gamatria multiple of terrestrial #4
$ץ^{90} ר^{200} א^1 ה^{5}$ $(1+5+200+90)$ =296=74 x 4,
4 compass points ("four corners") of the earth
Creation Day 4: lights/stars, celestial rule for; Signs, Seasons, Days, Years. (4 things)
Most basic three dimensional plane **geo**metric shape: Tetrahedron

5.   FIVE: GRACE, 3+2=5 Trinity-Completeness (3) plus
Marriage/difference (2) = Grace (5)
1+4=5 Celestial Unity extended to the 4 corners of the
terrestrial realm like the single apex or top of a pyramid (with
its 5 planes) shedding its rays over the 4-square garden plot of
the earth.
(3rd Prime Number)
The Hebrew word for *heavens* has a gematria that is a multiple
of 5;

Hashamayim ם ^{40} י ^{10} מ ^{40} שׁ ^{300} ה ^{5} = $^{40+10+40+300+5 = 395 \text{ or } 79x5}$

(by the way 79 = 23rd prime number = #of human chromosome pairs),

(5 is also a factor of the Tabernacle of Moses dimensions)
5 is the number of Grace; the Greek word for grace/gift
is *Charis*, χ^{600}α^{1}ρ^{100}ι^{10}ς^{200} or 600+1+100+10+200 = 911
Creation Day 5: moving water life, fowl, whales etc.
Five Kingdoms;
Mineral, Vegetable, Animal, Man, Celestial
Each kingdom reaches down into the lower realm below it but
cannot ascend into the higher kingdom above it.

6.   SIX: Number of man 3+3 = 6, rebellion,
multiples of time-limits on clock faces,
12 month calendars, and zodiacs
5+1 would be man's usurpation of Heaven
(our presumption on grace)
Creation Day 6: cattle, creeping things, beast, Man,
Dominion, names assigned &
Number 666 in Rev 13:18 is the "number of the beast". It is
also the number of "a man", created on the 6th day, living three
score (60) and ten years (Psalm 90:10) with four watches of 6
hours each.
A carbon-based life force made mostly of the 6th element, (AD
1860 = 310 x 6 = 6x6x51.666) (AD 1861= 6 x 310.1666)
Year of the War of the Great Rebellion (American Civil War)

7.   SEVEN: Number of Spiritual Perfection,
7 days a week, weeks of incubation/gestation, Rest
Number of rainbow colors ROYGBIV, Menorah
1st Law of Thermodynamics initiated
4th Prime Number)

8.   EIGHT: Number of Dominion, Regeneration,
Resurrection,
Musical octave, Eight day, the 1st day of a new week
Greek; Iesous is JESUS
$I^{10}\eta^8\sigma^{200}o^{70}\upsilon^{400}\sigma^{200}$ 10+8+200+70+400+200 = 888
8 = 2x2x2, 7+1,

9.   NINE: The Number of Judgment 3x3, final judgment
Cat-o-nine tails scourge, etc.
Pompeii & Herculaneum were destroyed by the eruption of Mt.
Vesuvius on August 24, 79 AD, exactly nine years after the
burning of Jerusalem.

10.   TEN: The Number of Ordinal Recommencement as 8 is
to 7 in weeks and musical octave

11.   ELEVEN: 12 minus 1 = Disorder *(5th Prime Number)*

12.   TWELVE: The Number of Governmental perfection;
12 Tribes, 12 Apostles, Hours of Time on clock face, Months
of the Year, Houses of the Zodiac

13.   THIRTEEN: The Number of rebellion, defection,
The first mention of 13 in Scripture is a rebellion *"Twelve
years they served Chedorlaomer, and in the thirteenth year
they rebelled."* (Gen. 14:4 & 17:25) Age of majority (Bar
mitzvah)
(6th Prime Number)

14.   FOURTEEN: Generations 2 x 7, (Weeks of gestation)
14 Generations from Abraham to David, 14 from David
to Babylon, 14 (13 human mortal) from Babylon to Jesus
Messiah. (Mt. 1:17)

15. FIFTEEN: See 3 x 5

16. SIXTEEN: See 4 x 4 etc.

17. SEVENTEEN: Spirit(7) + Order(10)
(7-4-1776? Revolution not rebellion)
(7ʰ Prime Number)

18. EIGHTEEN: See 3x6 and 9+9

19. NINETEEN: See 9 +10 *(8ᵗʰ Prime Number)*

20. TWENTY: See 2x10, 4x5, etc.

25. TWENTY-FIVE:= 5x5; multiplied grace

25. TWENTY-SIX: Gematrial value of the Tetragrammaton ה[5]ו[6]ה[5]י[10] Yaweh (Jehovah)

25. TWENTY-SEVEN: =3x3x3; Divine cube,

25. TWENTY-EIGHT: = 7x4;Spiritual perfection applied to the earth.

30. THIRTY: = 3x10 Divine Perfection (3) to order(10).

33. THIRTY-THREE: Age of Jesus at the Crucifixion (33 ½) Years David reigned in Jerusalem

40. FORTY: Number of Probation/trial
4x10 Order (10) brought down to earth(4)
Days it rained in the Flood of Noah
Days of Jesus' wilderness temptation
Years Israel wandered in the wilderness

Perfect numbers; 3x7x10x12 = 2,520 = 7x360 or 7 perfect Jewish years

Taken partially from:

E.W. Bullinger, **Number In Scripture**

Michael Hoggard, **By Divine Order**

F. W. Grant **Number in Scripture**

Appendix II.

The Digital Cube Root & Gematria of the Name of JESUS (ϑεσους)

ϑ ε σ ο υ σ

$10 + 8 + 200 + 70 + 400 + 200 =$ **888**

If we cube each of the integers of the number **888** we get **8** x **8** x **8** = 512 for each 8 in the number 888, the gematria value of the Greek name for Jesus.

$8^3+8^3+8^3 = 512 + 512 + 512 =$ **1536**
[1st operation]
If we again cube each of the integers of **1536** (the result above) we get:

$1^3+5^3+3^3+6^3 = 1 + 125 + 27 + 216 =$ **369**
[2nd operation]
If we do this cubing of each integer of 369 like the others we get

$3^3+6^3+9^3 = 27 + 216 + 729 = 972$
[3rd operation]
Cubing the individual integers of 972 and again adding them up together we get

$9^3+7^3+2^3 = 729 + 343 + 8 = 1080$
[4th operation]
Repeating the same process as before we get

$1^3+0^3+8^3+0^3 = 1 + 0 + 512 + 0 = 513$

[5th operation]

But now, on the 5th operation the next sum of the cubes of 513 will be the same as the sum of the cubes of 153 (or for that matter the other possible combinations of 315, 135, 531 or 351).

$5^3+1^3+3^3 = 125 + 1 + 27 = 153$

[6th operation]

(513 Resurrects to the transformed, stable, "immortal", number 153 on the sixth operation.)

$1^3+ 5^3+ 3^3 = 1 + 125 + 27 = 153$ etc.

[7th operation]

No new permutations are possible and the Gematrial cube root value of the precious name of Jesus rests on the seventh operation on precisely the same number of fishes caught in the net in John 21:11

*"**Simon Peter went up, and drew the net to land full of great fishes, an hundred and fifty and three: and for all there were so many, yet was not the net broken.**"*

This took place after the resurrection of the Lord Jesus Christ and is a picture of our resurrection with Him in an unbroken net.

No further transformations can take place on this immortal, resurrected, self-renewing number that points repeatedly back to our resurrected Savior as He stepped out of His rock-hewn tomb.

From Harrison, James, THE PATTERN AND THE PROPHECY

Number Puzzles and Personalities

STIGMA: 666

6	32	3	34	35	**1**
7	*11*	27	28	8	**30**
19	14	*16*	15	23	**24**
18	20	22	*21*	17	**13**
25	29	10	9	26	**12**
36	5	33	4	2	*31*

ANY SIX LINEAR ROWS COLUMNS OR DIAGONALS
ABOVE ADD TO 111

$6^2 = 36 = 6 \times 6$

(Every number below composes the chart above)

1+2+3+4+5+6+7+8+9+10+11+12+13+14+15+16+17+18+19+20+
21+22+23+24+25+26+27+28+29+30+31+32+33+34+35+36 = 666

The Sum of Every Roman Numeral = **666**

D=500

C=100 (M was not used in the ancient world. 2 C's=m)

  600   **600**

L=50

X=10

  60   **60**

V=5

I =1

  6   **+ 6**

        666

From out of nowhere; this is what happened when friars in the Middle Ages were denied television and movies.

Appendix IV

The Decalogue in the Periodic Table of the Elements

PERIODIC TABLE OF THE ELEMENTS

Our Creator has left His signature in the plan and organization of the substance of matter itself. He encoded from eternity past into the modern scientific terminology of the elements.

There is a hidden code embedded in the very structure of matter itself. This supernatural watermark emerged in the pattern of the Periodic Table of the Elements that first began to be deciphered by Mendeleev in the Nineteenth Century. It first became apparent to me at the turn of the 21st Century when my wife, Therese, noticed that the first ten elements of the Periodic Table fell into a pattern of both the Ten Commandments and the biblical symbolism of the numbers 1-10 as depicted in the list below.

Figure 11, The 1st ten elements of the periodic table

Element #1, [H], Hydrogen, is the most abundant element in outer-space, comprising more than ninety percent of the mass of the universe. It is the primal building block of matter. It also exists as one of three isotopes, Hydrogen, Deuterium, and Tritium; a Trinity of forms of the same most fundamental of all elements.

The number 1 is the symbol of commencement and unity in Scripture. On the first day of creation light, as in "point of light", appears. One is universally depicted in geometry as a single dot on the page or a single point in space.

The First Commandment requiring only One God is reiterated in the Lord's Prayer as *"Our Father in which art in Heaven"*[29] and corresponds with the singularity of Hydrogen in Heaven as a picture in nature of nature's God as the One Father of all who exists in the Trinity.

---

29   Matthew 6:9 and Luke 11:2

Element #2, [He], Helium, was named after the Greek sun god, Helios, because it was first detected in the light spectrum of the sun even before it was identified on earth. It is on the sun that Helium exists in highest concentration.

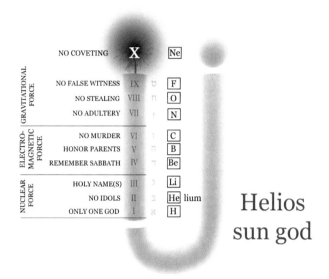

Helios sun god

The number 2 is the symbol of both division and multiplication or double mindedness vs. marriage in Scripture. In geometry this second point connected to the first point it copies defines a line in space, defining the second order of dimension; the straight line. The separation of these two points is a picture of the separation of the waters above from the waters below on the Second Day of creation.

The Second Commandment forbids idolatry and the worship of graven images. The most often idolized image in all the world over all time has been the sun where Helium is most abundant.

Element #3, [Li], Lithium, is named from the rock (*litho-*) in which it is found as an alkali metal. Lithium is the first of the remaining eight elements (of the ten we are considering here) listed in Period Two of the Periodic Table. This element and its next seven neighboring elements reside in the lower row just below the celestial elemental gases Hydrogen and Helium above.

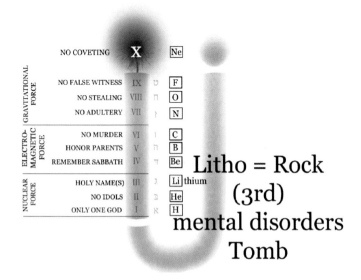

The number 3 is the number of completeness like the Trinity in Scripture. It takes three points to complete the first plane geometric shape on paper, the triangle. It was on the third day after Calvary that the resurrection took place just as the land rose up out of the water on the Third Day of creation.

Helium & Hydrogen (both with 3 syllables) in Period 1 exist above and apart from the lower periods just as these two primary gaseous elements are found as "spirits" up in outer space more than on earth; even as the Father and Holy Spirit exist above, distinct from, and as Holy Spirit over the material elements of the periods beneath them in the Periodic Table. Lithium (also 3 syllables) completes the trinity of the primary first three elements but appears in period 2 below in the realm of the ordinary material world just as Jesus was made flesh and dwelt among us as the material substance of the Trinity, the interface between the Godhead and mankind.

The Third Commandment is, "Not to take the Name of God in vain". That is why it is third, in order to designate how many names are holy. This commandment also conveys the notion of guilt. Guilt is the most common basis of mental disorders and the trinity of these disorders of mankind's fallen, guilty mind was described by the disciple Matthew.

"And his [Jesus'] *fame went throughout all Syria: and they brought unto him all sick people that were taken with divers diseases and torments, and those which were possessed with* **devils,** *and those which were* **lunatick,** *and those that had the* **palsy;** *and he healed them."* Matthew 4:24

The Lord Jesus Christ (as His Trinitarian Name reflects[30]), pointed out, as the Great Physician, that mental disorders could be classified under three categories that reflect the Trinitarian structure of our body, mind, and spirit. Palsy is a physical disorder. Lunacy is the loss of the mind's filter between body and spirit. Possession with devils is the substitution of the natural innate spirit of a person by an alien evil spirit.

It is interesting that Lithium compounds are still used extensively to treat manic-depressive mental disorders.

---

30   Lord = Father God King, Jesus = Yeshua Salvation, Christ = Messiah Anointed Spirit.

Element #4, [Be], Beryllium, a Group 2 alkali-**earth** metal, (ber-yll-i-um is a four syllable word).

The Fourth Commandment is "Remember the Sabbath to rest from the work you do on this **earth**".

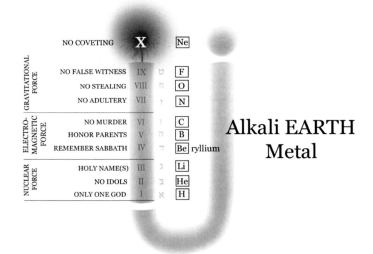

Alkali EARTH Metal

The number 4 is the number of terrestrial, created things "under the sun". 4 is the number that stands for the earth in Scripture; four corners, four cardinal compass points, four watches of the day, four seasons, four climatic regions etc.

Element #5, [B], Boron, a nearly inert, stable, semiconductor; it is a gracious mediator between metals and non-metals in the Periodic Table. Boron is so stable that it will not even react with boiling hydrochloric acid or boiling hydrofluoric acid (see the oxidizing viciousness of element #9 Fluorine below). Boron is most commonly found in borax, a cleansing compound that also makes a fine flux. Flux is used in welding, brazing, and soldering metals to keep them from oxidizing in the air as they are melted together. Borax acts as a gracious shield against the electron stealing and hording of Oxygen. See element #8 below.

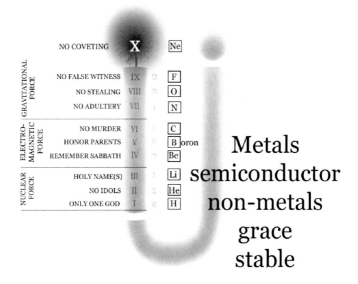

The number 5, as 4+1, is the number of God's grace shed from heaven at the apex of a five-surfaced five-pointed pyramid down onto its fifth surface a four-sided earthbound base. This is the square earth base we just encountered in the Fourth Commandment. The Fifth Commandment is to honor your father and mother that your days may be long on that four-sided earth-garden the Lord your God gives you. The gracious government of your parents is the most tolerance you are likely to ever encounter on the earth. Honoring our earthly father enables an understanding of our proper relationship with our Heavenly Father.

Element #6, [C], Carbon, is the most common and most important element in organic chemistry. Although carbon exists in the form of diamonds, the hardest matter found on earth, it is the organic chains, rings, helices, and other polymers of this simple atom that make it the most important element of all. Carbon is so important in every way that it was arbitrarily made the basis of all other atomic weights in 1964 when its atomic weight was re-assigned as exactly 12.000. We are all carbon-based life forms. All of our physical structure and the flesh of all plant and animal life, all known life anywhere is composed of hydrocarbon chains in three basic forms; proteins, carbohydrates, and fats. In addition to these three structural forms of carbon-chain molecules there are three more information forms of carbon-chain that occur in the form of a spiral helix; DNA, Transfer RNA, and Messenger RNA. Thus there are six forms of this sixth element that make life as we know it possible at all.

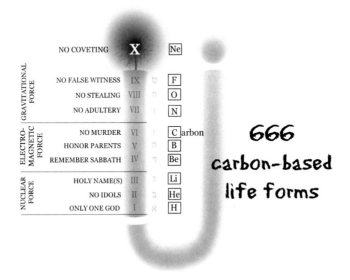

The number 6 is infamous in the Bible as "the number of a man", the Anti-Christ, 666. Adam was created on the sixth day.

Mankind rests on the seventh day from his six days of work each divided into four watches of six hours each. Psalm 90:10 notes that the days of our life add to three score (60) and ten years. The Sixth Commandment is "Thou shalt do no murder." and was the commandment violated at the Crucifixion with darkness that began at the sixth and lasted to the ninth[31] hour on 14th Nissan 3791/April 6th 30 AD. It is beyond coincidence that this most important element in the network of life should correspond with all of these biblical sixes.

---

31   9 is an inverted 6. Jesus was placed on the cross from the 3rd hour (9:00 am) to the 9th hour, which is 6 hours of His suffering on the cross as the Second Adam.

Element #7, [N], Nitrogen, comprises 78% of the atmosphere and is an integral part of the 22 amino acids that are the letters of protein sentences and peptide words that from our skin, muscle, bone and other structures and enzymes.

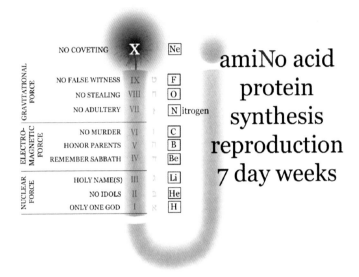

amiNo acid
protein
synthesis
reproduction
7 day weeks

7 is the number of spiritual perfection in Scripture and the work of the Holy Spirit as seen in the Seven Spirits of God around His throne and the Seven Lights on the Menorah and the transmission of the spirit of life in reproduction. Nitrogen occurs naturally as a gas, the spiritual state of matter.

The Seventh Commandment is against adultery, a violation of our Creator's covenant with us concerning reproduction and the transmission of the original spirit of lives first breathed into Adam. It is the Seventh Commandment because it governs the generation of life. Sexual reproduction takes place in all birds, insects, animals and humans in increments of weeks precisely; always exact multiples of seven days. The generation of life is the assembly of **nitrogen**-containing **amino** acids into proteins.

This protein synthesis in increments of seven-day weeks is also found in the record of the lineage of Jesus the Messiah in the first chapter of Matthew where there are 14 generations from Abraham to David[32], 14 from David to the Babylonian Captivity, and 14 generations from Babylon to Jesus.

---

32 The Hebrew for "David" DVD ד ו ד has a numerical value of ד (4) + ו (6) + ד (4) = 14.

Element #8, [O], Oxygen, occurs also as a gas without which no life as we know it could exist. It is the most useful and important drug in Cardio-Pulmonary-Resuscitation.

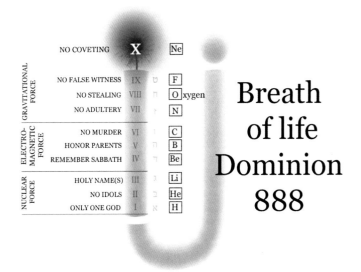

8 is the d**O**minical number of Jesus and His Name who's New Testament Greek spelling Ιησους gamatria totals 888 (or the Trinity number 111 x 8). It is the 1st day of the new week or the 8th day on which the Lord resurrected, commencing His Dominion over death and time in the calendar terminology, **AD**, "**A**nno **D**omini"; Year of Our Lord.

The Eighth Commandment prohibits steeling, thus assuring our dominion over our own personal property. It is interesting that in chemistry the ideal valence or number of electrons in the outer shell of the 10 elements we are examining seems to be eight electrons. Oxygen has two electrons in the lowest energy shell nearest the nucleus and only six in the next shell that prefers to have eight. Oxygen "steals" an electron from each of two hydrogen atoms to form water H_2O. (There is more to this element that has escaped us so far that hinges on the anti-oxidant effect of macronutrients.)

Element #9, [F], Fluorine, is a halogen or salt-forming element at the far upper right extreme of the periodic table's oxidative or corrosive elements. Fluorine is the single worst corrosive agent known and even burns water. (Even boiling hydrofluoric acid fails to corrode the grace element #5, boron, or alter any of the noble gases such as Helium and the 10th element, Neon.)

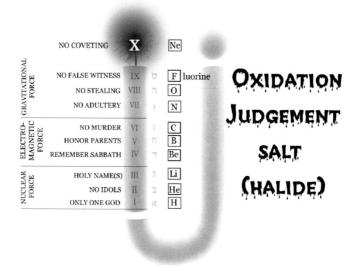

The number 9, as 3 x 3, represents the product of divine completeness and the finality of a trinity of trinities, the ultimate judgment of God. This is not only seen in Scripture but it is illustrated in historical events such as the divine retribution and judgment of God on the Roman Empire and Caesar for the destruction of Jerusalem in August of 70 AD (9th of Av). Nine years after Emperor Vespasian's son, Titus, burned the Temple in Jerusalem Vesuvius erupted near 9 AM on an August morning in 79 AD and buried Pompeii and Herculaneum, the two wealthiest cities in the empire. That same ninth year after Jerusalem was destroyed, Vespasian died, having failed to finish the Coliseum from the spoils of Jerusalem. God's judgment fell upon Rome nine years after Rome destroyed Jerusalem.

The Ninth Commandment is, *"Thou shalt not bear false witness against thy neighbor"*. This crime is most heinous and has its worst effect when committed before the judgment seat in court, where the victim may lose their property (commandment 8), their spouse (commandment 7), or their life (commandment 6). It is a far-reaching and corrosive violation that is identical to the corrosion of fluorine. It is interesting that this corrosive action of the Ninth Element and Commandment is only impossible on boron, element #5, the number of grace and the Noble Gas Helium that symbolizes the Holy Spirit. The corrosion by fluorine is prevented by immersion in one of the noble gases in Group 18 such as our final example, Neon.

Element #10, [Ne], Neon, is one of the Noble Gases, the first of which, Helium, we have already encountered. The Noble Gases are as nearly inert and un-reactive as any finite physical material can be. They are called "Noble" because of their resistance to reactions with any other element.

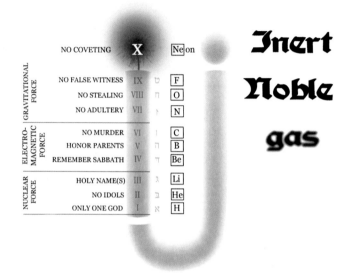

The number 10 represents recommencement of numeration in the base ten just as eight stands for the first day of a new week in the base seven. Thus not lighting off the 10th Commandment is a better way to keep out of the other nine judgmental commandments.

The Tenth Commandment is, *"Thou shalt not covet."* It is the only commandment where violation alone affects nobody else except the violator. It is a thought crime that controls the will. It is the most noble and superior of the Ten Commandments because, although the least in effect and least obvious in its keeping it is the fuse that lights off the rest of the other nine commandments. If you don't want to break a commandment by avoiding the covet fuse, it will not blow up in your face. It is only accomplished by putting down the old man we are born with and *"letting this mind which was also in Christ Jesus"[33]* take over.

The same Creator that spoke the substance of the universe into existence and who formed Adam from the dust of the earth (dust ordered out in the Periodic Table of the Elements) also encoded within the system of numbers and the Ten Commandments a watermark that links His material works with His Word. Jesus was, is and will be our Rock of Ages; made of the dust of the earth just as the first Adam yet without sin. Jesus the Messiah was seen in the Torah as the same Rock that Moses was only to have struck once at Horeb, but not again at Kaddish Barnea; the same Rock in who's cleft Moses hid himself on Mt. Sinai from the fierce energy of the Father; the same Rock where Jesus' sedimentary rock tomb was cut out of Jerusalem limestone and like the buried fossils of matter in that sedimentary rock rose from his grave that we might have eternal life at our own resurrection.

---

33   Philippians 2:5

Appendix V

THE GENETIC CODE

ADENINE				
DNA Base CodeS	Messenger RNA Mirror	Amino Acid	Abbrev-	Listed Order
AAA -	(UUU) -	Phenylalanine	Phe F	14th
AAC -	(UUG) -	Leucine	Leu L	11th
AAG -	(UUC) -	Phenylalanine	Phe F	14th
AAT -	(UUA) -	Leucine	Leu L	11th
ACA -	(UGU) -	Cysteine	Cys C	5th
ACC -	(UGG) -	Tryptophan	Trp W	18th
ACG -	(UGC) -	Cysteine	Cys C	5th
ACT -	(UGA) -	STOP Codon		
AGA -	(UCU) -	Serine	Ser S	16th
AGC -	(UCG) -	Serine		
AGG -	(UCC) -	Serine		
AGT -	(UCA) -	Serine		
ATA -	(UAU) -	Tyrosine	Tyr Y	19th
ATC -	(UAG) -	STOP Codon		
ATG -	(UAC) -	Tyrosine	Tyr Y	19th
ATT -	(UAA) -	STOP Codon		

CYTOSINE				
DNA Base CodeS	Messenger RNA mirror	Amino Acid	Abbrev-	Listed Order
CAA -	(GUU) -	Valine	Val V	20th
CAC -	(GUG) -	Valine		
CAG -	(GUC) -	Valine		
CAT -	(GUA) -	Valine		
CCA -	(GGU) -	Glycine	Gly G	8th
CCC -	(GGG) -	Glycine		
CCG -	(GGC) -	Glycine		
CCT -	(GGA) -	Glycine		
CGA -	(GCU) -	Alanine	Ala A	1st
CGC -	(GCG) -	Alanine		
CGG -	(GCC) -	Alanine		
CGT -	(GCA) -	Alanine		
CTA -	(GAU) -	Aspartic Acid	Asp D	4th
CTC -	(GAG) -	Glutamic Acid	Glu E	6th
CTG -	(GAC) -	Aspartic Acid	Asp D	4th
CTT -	(GAA) -	Glutamic Acid	Glu E	6th

GUANINE				
DNA Base Codes	Messenger RNA Mirror	Amino Acid	Abbrev-	Listed Order
GAA -	(CUU) -	Leucine	Leu L	11th
GAC -	(CUG) -	Leucine		
GAG -	(CUC) -	Leucine		
GAT -	(CUA) -	Leucine		
GCA -	(CGU) -	Arginine	Arg R	2nd
GCC -	(CGG) -	Arginine		
GCG -	(CGC) -	Arginine		
GCT -	(CGA) -	Arginine		
GGA -	(CCU) -	Proline	Pro P	15th
GGC -	(CCG) -	Proline		
GGG -	(CCC) -	Proline		
GGT -	(CCA) -	Proline		
GTA -	(CAU) -	Histidine	His H	9th
GTC -	(CAG) -	Glutamine	Gln Q	7th
GTG -	(CAC) -	Histidine	His H	9th
GTT -	(CAA) -	Glutamine	Gln Q	7th

THYMINE (THYMIDINE)				
DNA Base Codes	Messenger RNA Mirror	Amino Acid	Abbrev-	Listed Order
TAA -	(AUU) -	Isoleucine	Ile I	10th
TAC -	(AUG) -	Methionine	Met M	13th
TAG -	(AUC) -	Isoleucine	Ile I	10th
TAT -	(AUA) -	Isoleucine	Ile I	10th
TCA -	(AGU) -	Serine	Ser S	16th
TCC -	(AGG) -	Arginine	Arg R	2nd
TCG -	(AGC) -	Serine	Ser S	16th
TCT -	(AGA) -	Arginine	Arg R	2nd
TGA -	(ACU) -	Threonine	Thr T	17th
TGC -	(ACG) -	Threonine		
TGG -	(ACC) -	Threonine		
TGT -	(ACA) -	Threonine		
TTA -	(AAU) -	Asparagine	Asn N	3rd
TTC -	(AAG) -	Lysine	Lys K	12th
TTG -	(AAC) -	Asparagine	Asn N	3rd
TTT -	(AAA) -	Lysine	Lys K	12th

The Alphabet of Amino Acids
Polypeptide Words & Protein Sentences

1. Alanine, Ala A

2. Arginine, Arg R

3. Asparagine, Asn N

4. Aspartic acid, Asp D

5. Cysteine, Cys C

6. Glutamic acid, Glu E

7. Glutamine, Gln Q

8. Glycine, Gly G

9. Histidine, His H

10. Isoleucine, Ile I

11. Leucine, Leu L

12. Lysine, Lys K

13. Methionine, Met M

14. Phenylalanine, Phe F

15. Proline, Pro P

16. Serine, Ser S

17. Threonine, Thr T

18. Tryptophan, Trp W

19. Tyrosine, Tyr Y

20. Valine, Val V

21. *Hydroxy Proline,* (Structural component of cartilage)

22. *Gamma Amino* Butyric Acid, (GABA), a neurotransmitter

Appendix VI

Vowel Points

In the list of vowel points below any generic consonant is indicated as an X with the vowel points sprinkled around it like salt and pepper. They are very small so we have expanded the font size on this page.

a as in y**a**cht, פַ תַ ה *Patah* Xַ

& קָ מָ ץ *Qames* Xָ

ee as in s**ee**, הִ י ֶר ק *Hireq* Xִ & Xִי

ay as in h**ay**, צֵ רֵ י *Tzere* Xֵ & Xֵי

eh as in b**e**d, סֶ ג ו ל *Segol* Xֶ

e as in stup**e**fy הֳ טָף קָ מָ ץ *Hataf Qames* Xֳ

o as in r**o**w, ה ו לָ ם *Holem* Xֹ & Xוֹ

oo as in z**oo**, קֻ בוֹץ *Quibbus* Xֻ

& שׁ ו ר ק *Shureq* Xוּ

שׁ ָ ו א The *Sheva* X□

Bibliography

Blech, Benjamin, Rabbi

THE SECRETS OF THE HEBREW WORDS
1991, Jason Aronson Inc.
230 Livingston St. Northvale, N.J. 07647
ISBN 0-87668-610-2, ISBN 1-56821-918-0

MORE SECRETS OF THE HEBREW WORDS,
Holy Days & Happy Days
1993, Jason Aronson Inc.
ISBN 0-87668-223-9

Bullinger, Ethelbert William, Rev. 1837-1913

NUMBER IN SCRIPTURE
1898, Republished 1967 Kregel Publications
P.O. Box 2607, Grand Rapids, Mi. 49501
ISBN 0-8254-2238-8

Drosnin, Michael

THE BIBLE CODE
© 1997 Michael Drosnin
1997, Simon & Schuster
Rockefeller Center
1230 Avenue of the Americas
New York, New York 10020
ISBN 0-684-81079-4

Grant, F.W.

THE NUMERICAL STRUCTURE OF SCRIPTURE
1887, 12th Printing 1989 Loizeaux Brothers
Neptune, New Jersey
ISBN 0-87213-269-2
The Numerical Bible

Green, Jay P., Sr. General Editor & Translator

THE INTERLINEAR BIBLE
Hebrew-Greek-English
1976-'86 Hendrickson Publishers
Peabody, Massachusetts 01961-3473
ISBN 0-913573-25-6

Harrison, James, 1936-

THE PATTERN AND THE PROPHECY
1996, 1st ed. Isaiah Publications
P.O. Box 1221, Peterborough Ontario,
Canada K9J7H4
http://www.ptbo.igs.net/~isaiah/
(800) 537-5489, Fax (705) 741-1444
ISBN 0-9698512-0-0

Kang, C. H. & Ethyl R. Nelson M.D.

THE DISCOVERY OF GENESIS
How the truths of Genesis were found hidden in the
Chinese Language
1979 Concordia Publishing House
3558 South Jefferson Ave. St. Louis, Mo. 63118
ISBN 0-570-03792-1

McBirnie, William Steuart, Ph.D.

(B.A., B.D., M.R.E., D.R.E., Th.D., D.D., F.R.G.S., O.S.J.)

THE SEARCH FOR THE AUTHENTIC TOMB OF JESUS,
1975 Third Printing Abridged 1981
Acclaimed Books
P.O. Box 585, Montrose, California, 91020
(Currently suppressed and out of print)

Morris, Henry M. Ph.D.

THE GENESIS RECORD
1976 Baker Book House, Grand Rapids, Michigan
& Creation-Life Publishers, San Diego, California
ISBN 0-89051-026-1

Mozeson, Isaac E.

THE WORD, The Dictionary that reveals Hebrew Sources
of English
© 1995 Isaac E. Mozeson (201) 836-3410
693 Chestnut Av. Teaneck N.J. 07666
25/6 Yehoshua Bin Nun, Jerusalem Israel,
telephone 02/638-851
Jason Aronson Inc.
230 Livingston St., Northvale, New Jersey 07647
ISBN 1-56821-615-7

Nelson, Ethel R., M.D. & Richard E. Broadberry

GENESIS AND THE MYSTERY CONFUCIUS COULDN'T SOLVE
1986, Revised 1994 Concordia Publishing House
ISBN 0-570-04635-1

Parkhurst, Rev. John, M.A. 1728-1797

A HEBREW AND ENGLISH LEXICON WITHOUT POINTS
William Baynes & Son, Paternoster Row
London, England
Out of Print (1823 reprint of 1765 Ed. cited here)

Rambsel, Yacov

YESHUA, The Name of Jesus Revealed in the Old Testament
1996, Frontier Research Publications
P.O. Box 470470, Tulsa, Ok 74147-0470
Harmony Printing Ltd. Canada
ISBN 0-921714-34-3

HIS NAME IS JESUS, The Mysterious Yeshua Codes
© 1997 Yacov A. Rambsel
Frontier Research Publications
ISBN 0-921714-00-9

Satinover. Jeffrey, M.D.

CRACKING THE BIBLE CODE, © 1997
William Morrow & Co. N.Y.
1350 Avenue of The Americas
New York, New York, 10019
ISBN 0-688-15463-8

Simon, Resnikoff, Motzin

THE FIRST HEBREW PRIMER
1995 3rd Edition EKS Publishing Company
5346 College Ave.
Oakland, California 94618
ISBN 0-939144-15-8

Washburn, Del & Jerry Lucas
THEOMATICS: God's best kept secret revealed
©1977 Jerry Lucas & Del Washburn
Stein and Day/publishers/Scarborough house,
Briarcliff Manor, N.Y. 10510
ISBN 0-8128-2181-5

Young, Robert, LL.D.
ANALYTICAL CONCORDANCE TO THE BIBLE
Hendrickson Publishers
Peabody, Massachusetts 01961-3473
ISBN 0-917006-29-1

About The Author

Dr. Chuck Thurston and Therese, his lovely wife for 49 years, were the hosts for many years of WRFD Radio's "Evidences - Think Radio" a live call-in Christian apologetics talk show on Salem Radio. Dr. Thurston is an instrument rated and multi-engine pilot and has made numerous medical mission trips to most of the places and terrible conditions (featured in the recent motion picture "The Sound of Freedom") like Haiti, Honduras, Belize, Guatemala, and Mexico serving with Y.W.A.M., Mercy Ships, Sharing Ministries, World Harvest for Christ, Operation Blessing, Heart to Honduras, and the Baptist River Ministry along the Rio Grande over the years.

This doctor is also an accomplished blacksmith, cabinet-maker, and Eighteenth Century gunsmith. He has used these skills and his forge and shop to make models of the Wilderness Tabernacle of Moses. Other books by the author include, "In His Image" and a medical text, "Cancer Terminology For Medical Students".

A board-certified emergency physician, Dr. Thurston has served in over 100 hospitals in a dozen States and nearly as many foreign countries for five decades.

Dr. Thurston is the President and founder of Evidences Biblical Institute, that seeks to find answers in both the Word of God and the works of God to the hard questions about mankind's origins, purpose, and our destiny. Dr. Chuck Thurston and Therese, his lovely wife for 39 years, were the hosts from 1999 to 2005 of WRFD Radio's *"Evidences"*, a weekly call-in Christian apologetics talk show in Worthington, Ohio. The Thurstons have two sons, David and Andrew, in college and they all live on a farm near Chillicothe, Ohio. The farm doubles as the runway for Mission Field Aviation. Dr. Thurston is an instrument rated and multi-engine pilot and has made numerous medical missions trips to Haiti, Honduras, Belize, Guatemala, and Mexico serving with Y.W.A.M., Sharing Ministries, World Harvest for Christ, Operation Blessing, Heart to Honduras, and the Baptist River Ministry along the Rio Grande over the years.

Evidences

Dr. Thurston is the President and founder of **Evidences** Biblical Institute, where *"The Bible is the Living Word of God...and we can prove it!"* Topics for discussion and scholarly investigation have included, *Creation-Evolution, Apparent Contradictions in Scripture, Archaeological Discoveries, Quantum Physics, Astro-physics, the Age of the Earth, the Bible Codes, Mathematical Patterns in Scripture and Nature, Genetics and the Virgin Birth*, just to mention only a few. Evidences Biblical Institute seeks to find answers in both the Word of God and the works of God to the hard questions about mankind's origins, purpose, and our destiny.

© March 19, 2000
Pocket Edition © June 22, 2007
Reprinted September 2023
Charles Jenkins Thurston M.D.
Evidences Biblical Institute
13316 Marietta Rd.
Kingston, Ohio 45644
(740) 655-2626
chuck@evidences.net

www.evidences.net
www.doozy.tv
www.medical-opinions.com
www.ScienceAndWonders.com

The Wizard of Id cartoon was sent to me as a postcard by Yacov Rambsel and used by permission from Johnny Hart just before they both went home to be with The Lord.